RECIPROCITY

Edward Cunningham

By: Edward Cunningham
Created and Published by: City of Jabez, Jabez
Publishing House, Remnant Books
Designed by: City of Jabez

Copyright Disclaimer

U.S. Library of Congress Registration Catalog

This book or parts thereof may not be reproduced in any form, stored in a retrieval system, or transmitted in any form by any means— electronic, mechanical, photocopy, recorded, or otherwise—without prior written permission of the publisher, except as provided by the United States of America copyright law. Biblical Reference Unless otherwise noted, scripture references were taken from the King James Version of the Holy Bible.

ISBN: 978-1-7369155-6-1

Copyright 2021© by Edward Cunningham. All Rights Reserved.

Contents

Dedication	5
Preface	7
Introduction	7
Evolution of the 21st Century Woman	17
Laws of Polarity	30
The Octopus Man	49
Top 5 Needs of Man and Woman	53

The Level 3 needs of a Woman	65
Levels 2 and 3 needs of a Man	68
The Levels 4 and 5 needs of men and women	76
Physiology of Attraction	80
Technology Policy	96
Ladies and Gentlemen	105
Laws of Zero	111

Dedication

I dedicate this book to my parents because of the foundational tools that were provided in my upbringing. Without adequate foundational tools, the process of building anything in life becomes increasingly more arduous. The unyielding trust, support, and autonomy to do whatever I wanted will always have a place in my heart.

In addition, I dedicate this to all my readers. Just the fact that you have read this book lets me know that you are trying to make a difference in your life. If my research and experience can help one relationship then I have helped a family. If I helped a family then I have proliferated joy.

PREFACE

Introduction

Author Edward Cunningham identifies relevant and significant tools that help maintain and rejuvenate relationships that may lackluster, passion, and desire.

The word reciprocity comes from a French word 1766, from French *réciprocité* (18c.), from *reciproque*, from Latin *reciprocus*, past participle of *reciprocare* (see **reciprocal**). To give and take.

I want to first thank you for supporting the book "Reciprocity". Twenty years of personal study and research in an attempt to add layers of improvement to myself and my relationships have been revealed in this book Reciprocity. The core focus of my work lies primarily in personal relationships. You will discover that many of the relationship laws and principles outlined in this book apply to every aspect of your life. Our society is currently positioned in the middle of a social paradigm shift. I had no desire to write this book until I was asked by countless credible individuals who thought that the overall approach was very effective. This book was written to offer an alternative perspective from traditional relationship management. Many of the terms such as the "C" scale, 5 top needs of women, 5 top needs of men, needs assessment point system, octopus man, cicada woman, industrial man, and many more are all original. This is why the book is so in-depth because life is complicated. If you are looking for a paragraph or 2 and walk back in your relationship hoping for a change you have the wrong book. Reciprocity is a universal law that encompasses every aspect of our lives from what we eat, drink, exercise, education, economically, environmentally, spiritually, and beyond. All of these factors have a direct impact on the overall health of our relationships. 100% of the information provided has been referenced and researched over the years in conjunction with personal experience. Connecting the dots in human physiology, psychology, polarity and their role in our relationship decision making is paramount. I believe that this book will enhance relationships that are looking to reignite the fire and juice you once had. It is also possible to rekindle relationships that may be at the fringes of despair. Let me first disclose that I have been indulged in marriage twice in my life. First marriage (15) years and my second is active 12 years together and 5.5 years married. I've owned 10 businesses managed over 250 employees, 4 years of college that ranged from computer science, fire science, and hydraulics. Raised 2 boys, a daughter and my 3-year-old is a work in progress. I've distributed the teachings and administered "Robert Rhome" personality profiles to my agents and employees on over 200 occasions. Personally, I was administered the class in Mississauga, Canada in 2004. Also, I am a high "D" personality, in case you are interested. Leaders by nature and extremely task-oriented. I had an impeccable childhood thanks to perpetually loving parents who gave me the autonomy to explore and live life on my terms. A middle-class household, where mom never used profanity and dad never said no to anyone. We traveled, bowled, skied, swam, and participated every sport imaginable. I am, without question, the by-product of my upbringing. I've never indulged in drugs and never been mind-altered from alcohol. A couple of light drinks and I've reached capacity. I run 12 miles a week with my 3-year-old son in his stroller. I try to eat nutritionally beneficial foods that are organic-based and free of preservatives. I will stop here because this is not a biography of Edward Cunningham, but I felt compelled to give you

INTRODUCTION

a snapshot of my background and how I try to live my life. My current relationship if I were to make an assessment is passionate, purposeful, and fulfilling at every level possible. Most successful relationships have a comfortable balance physiologically, economically, politically, socially, environmentally, and spiritually. There is an entire physiological ecosystem on a cellular level that has a significant influence on our emotions, motivation, and desire. I will go into this more in the chapter "physiology of attraction". I could not read a relationship book authored by someone who has never been married. I think the task to convey the challenges that exist when you commit your life to another individual contractually without ever being immersed in the process is arduous and cannot to effectively empathize with couples who are indulged in long-term relationships. This would be like me conducting an alcohol anonymous meeting knowing that I've never been intoxicated in life. I'm the guy that drives home the inebriated after the party. Also, I think that it can be challenging for relationship coaches who have not been married or committed for any significant time. I'm not suggesting that they are ineffective, but let's be realistic, our mind and body go through spiritual changes every seven years starting at conception. The number 7 is used in the great book 735 times. How can you assess a long-term relationship health if you don't have an experience beyond the incipient levels of relationship development? Let me go on record before I start and disclose that I do not have a perfect relationship, in fact, no one does. If you believe you have a perfect relationship then you possibly have more of a dictatorship because someone is in a full-time compliance mode. Identical twins who have the same set of 23 chromosomes that make up who they are will develop over time different personalities primarily because life can't ensure that their experiences and perceptions will occur at the same time. This will overtime have a direct impact on the overall development of all four quadrants of the brain. The reason I mention this is to shed light on the fact that you will never get anyone to agree with everything that you desire in life, so stop looking. I have learned over the years that it's not always about how well you get along, but more about how well you argue. Good relationships argue well. I can tell you that I met my wife 12 years ago and I am just as passionate about her existence today as I was when we first met. I want to also say that one of the first things I told my wife when we decided to commit our lives together was "Your existence is not necessary for the survival of my internal happiness," as her eyes got bigger, I said "let me divulge...I would never be so selfish to make my happiness your responsibility". However, "I feel tremendously empowered and supported with you in my life". Furthermore, I need you to enhance and provide me with the tools that I don't possess in my arsenal and collectively if we consolidate our energies, ideas and love we can become a greater force that can overcome any problem and accomplish anything the world has to offer. I am sure through my efforts; I can enhance you as well. If you were to leave, it would be a sad day in my life and probably take significant time to overcome. The reason for this sadness is because you are a true asset to me. If you were not an asset you could only be a liability. People celebrate the removal of liabilities. I will go over more of this in the chapters "Laws of Zero" and "Polarity". I figured out a long time ago that relationships don't end because of the lack of love, they most often end because of the lack of passion and intimacy precipitated by the neglect of primary needs not being met. If you listen to many divorced couples, many would say that you know I still love and care for "John" but we have irreconcilable differences. Translation, he went one way mentally and I went the other. The couple failed to make love language adjustments and eventually all of the oil burned out of the jar and the wick lost its flame. The failure to maintain and identify the fundamental needs of masculine energy versus feminine energy will cause your relationship to go into a downward spiral. I will identify that later in the chapter "Physiology of Emotions". Most of the material on relationships that I have read in the past failed to connect the matrix between physiology and principles. A Recent study found that 38% of married couples who participated in marital counseling got divorced or separated within 5 years post counseling. Let me give you an example. If you take a quick break right now and ask your child (if you have one). "Why should you get good grades in school?" The answers that I received were, "because you told me too", "So I can graduate", "So I can get on the honor roll". Older children will say things like, "so I can get in a good college or university". My point is that the failure to connect the inner psychological dots means that you can never discover your purpose. I had to get that out because I had to create an illustration for my daughter in middle school. After all, she had no idea why grades were so important. She thought that getting good grades was exclusively a parental achievement. I created a chart and on the left side, I listed no education, GED, Diploma, Associate Degree, Bachelor's degree, Doctorate or pursue the entrepreneur side if you have the courage. On the right side, I listed the projected income based on the value that her effort would produce later in life. On the right side next to (no education), I listed low-paying minimum wage positions and how much money was necessary to obtain the things that she wanted in life. I made a correlation without any force that money does not follow people, money only follows value. If you want to make more money than you must first increase your value. I never talked to her about grades again at any time in life. She was so afraid of living in destitute that she scored 1380 on the SAT and received 2 academic scholarships from St John's University in New York where she currently attends. So, I know you are wondering what does your daughter has to do with relationship principles. I'm drawing comparisons to the fact that anything in life that you have an overwhelming desire to have, must have Purpose, Passion, and Capacity. Reciprocity works very similarly. If you want someone in your life that is capable of stimulating you mentally in your relationship, don't you think it's important to first work on increasing your value. I don't mean from a monetary perspective but rather increasing self-worth by first making a self-analysis on your deficiencies which we all have. My son's name is Kaizen which means constant and perpetual improvement. I know I veered off the relationship path momentarily but it was necessary to back you into my attempt to connect the internal wiring that exist synergistically with masculine energy and feminine energy. One of the most daunting tasks the average person will be exposed to in a lifetime is the management of marriage and money. Unfortunately, relationships don't come with owner's manuals. We have become so arrogant to the point that we will read the owner's manual of our new smartphone, but invest no time on relationship principles and management. Fast forward 7 years and you have developed a disdain for someone you once adored. We are faced with the value and belief systems that were available during our upbringing. It was the Greek philosopher Aristotle before 322 BC said "GIVE ME A CHILD UNTIL HE IS SEVEN AND I WILL SHOW YOU THE MAN". Mark Twain said, "DON'T LET YOUR SCHOOLING INTERFERE WITH YOUR EDUCATION". Were these guys fantastic or not? I reference these quotes because we fight so often in relationships over so much that was created and formulated deep inside the neurons of past experiences. We obtain a degree and believe that we are fully educated. Let me tell you that there is a fundamental difference between education and intelligence. Education is associated more with external learning and memorization, but intelligence has to do more with one's internal learning and decision making. How many politicians with bachelor's and master's degrees have been prosecuted and convicted over the years? The answer is "a lot". The education is present but the intelligence is deficient. Many of us, once we complete our commencement exercises don't study anything else in life unless it's associated with making more money. The word commencement means the beginning of something, not the end. Our brain frequencies are primarily dominated in delta, theta waves before four years of age. These are states of a deep sleep, dreaming, hypnosis, and mental downloads of our environment. A significant part of our personality is formed during this growth period. My son sees me every day kissing my wife with every purpose and passion and he is only three. Do you think that this will have an impact on how he views marriage later in life? Do you think that he is learning how to treat someone he love? If you frequently fight, argue or exhibit high levels of dysfunction in the presence of children, they will tend to develop a negative perspective on the word commitment later in life because of the lack of positive references. This may be the reason that we tend to create the relationship learning manuals as we go and hope that it works. Can you imagine buying a new car and figuring out at 50,000-mile mark that you should have been changing the oil every three thousand miles? You take it to the shop because you have blue smoke coming out of the exhaust. The damage in many cases is irreversible. By the time you figure out half of what you are doing the hormonal glue that got you together has been so depleted that the relationship has entered into a dark precarious zone with no direction or purpose. I will share my reasoning later in the book under the chapter, "Laws of Chokra's". I would be remised if I did not include health, finance, wellness, psychology, sociology, and most of all your god. I have to leave it at your god because there are over 6000 religions and over 600 versions of the bible that currently exist. I don't have the time or energy to get into any political or religious debate. I would like to also add that this book will be less effective for relationships where one or both persons partake in irrational behavior that may include promiscuity, drug, alcohol abuse, unmedicated and untreated bipolar disorders, depression, chronic, verbal, and or physical abuse, etc. I make this distinction because there is no book created in modern history that has the answer to all of life's challenges. It's tough enough managing a sober relationship, when you add external substances the conscious mind becomes distorted and rational thinking becomes ineffective. I think for best results individuals who desire to have a long healthy relationship filled with purpose and passion will find the information extremely useful. Those of you who are indulged in your singleness will benefit the most because you get the opportunity to set parameters in the incipient stages of your relationship to create a healthy culture that will proliferate for generations to come. People who are in existing relationships have to eradicate the ineffective habits and implement new relationship strategies.

My quest over the last 20 years of studying psychology, physiology, sociology, economics, money principles primarily evolved because of my desire to understand myself and others. When 100 CEOs of fortune 500 companies were asked, "What is the most important quality that you look for in a leader" the answer overwhelmingly was people skills. I was committed to not live in a loveless household filled with pain, dejection, and embarrassment. My commitment to maintaining a consistent level of lust and infatuation for my life partner became the highest priority. Learning who I was and my purpose for existing had to be my number one priority. I knew that if I found my purpose that passion would soon follow. Fire for example must have fuel, heat, and oxygen to burn. The removal of any of the three elements will certainly cause the fire to self-extinguish. The removal of purpose, passion, or capacity out of any of your endeavors will create great resistance and possible failure. What shapes our behavior is love. Men don't typically talk about their relationships at the level that women do. I don't have any male associates in my circle that read maintenance books on relationships. We don't ask for directions and we certainly don't ask for advice on our relationships. I asked a friend how was the family doing and he said that he and his wife can't stand each other, in fact, they slept in separate rooms for the last year. I said you guys used to talk on the phone until one of you fell asleep. They still at work the same jobs, have the same children, bills are paid so what happen? She said "he often sends flower to her job". He said, "he has not seen his wife in lingerie in 5 years". I will dive deeper into the chapter "Reciprocity". I will talk about the stress hormone cortisol and how it affects your health and relationships in the chapter Physiology of Emotions. It would behoove of you to manage stress levels that often surface in relationships for your own physical and mental health. Understand every level of growth in life has its own set of unique challenges. In most cases, the primary reason for most relationship turmoil is the fact that needs are not being met. My study has revealed that the national divorce rate is between 30-40 % depending on your sources. Statistically, women file 70 percent of all divorces in the US. Many couples never spent enough time dating themselves experiencing who you are. The need and thirst to have companionship is often desired to conceal insecurities within the confines of our inner soul. Your armor has been compromised since you were a child. The pain seeps through the cracks causing decay in your heart. You never rectified the problem and fast forward 20 or 30 years and you get married to a person that you don't know. Your insecurities cause you to panic with the thought of being alone, so you commit to a relationship with no relevant criteria during the vetting and qualification process. One thing the creator wanted to ensure was propagation. If you see something that you are attracted to, the body with no effort on your part reacts chemically by secreting high levels of dopamine and testosterone for men, dopamine, and oxytocin in women. What keeps us from acting on every impulse is primarily our value and belief system embedded deep in our conscious mind. You have been chemically hypnotized during the lust and infatuation period and often ask yourself where are all the good men or women. Remember you attract who you are. The energy that you exude daily may be so toxic that the pheromones and electrical vibrations can't synergize with anything of relevance or importance. So, you settle for a person that you think you love. Your love criteria were so fragmented that they lacked structure, standards, and values. You could not possibly have your sorority sisters or frat brothers see you alone. Your criteria centered around filling life voids and empty caverns rather than relationships morals, values, and beliefs. You had no idea that love was not just a feeling, but it's also a behavior and a responsibility. You dared to get married under the presumption that good sex, dates, gifts, trips, and a marital contract were all that was needed for perpetual love. You were under the impression that lust and infatuation would never fade. Once the neurotransmitters and hormones subsided the glue that held your relationship together dissipated like a thief in the night. You never knew that your entire relationship was built on a hormonal foundation which is much like trying to build a high-rise building on beach sand. You possess no rational relationship tools that would give you any chance to maintain the novelty in the relationship. As you journey through this book you will discover that this book took 20 years of research and personal experience. Reciprocity will attempt to shed light on you and your contribution to your own life through waves, energy, and vibrations. Aligning yourself with the people and energies that are conducive to who you are. We spend too much time concerned about what someone is not doing for us and feeling shortchanged. Someone asks me, "Edward, what if I do all of this and they never respond?" The world without much effort has an amazing way of realigning our energies and vibrations with other stars. Remember the only thing in life that you have complete control of is you. It took me 30 years before I realized that you can't motivate people you can only inspire them. Motivation is an internal force that has to come from within, influenced chemically through neurotransmitters and hormones.

I want to thank you again for your support and I hope that my research and experiences that I have shared can offer you beneficial information in a variety of ways that can help enhance your life psychologically, physiologically, economically, and spiritually.

Evolution of the 21st Century Woman

Someone once said that the greatest weapon of an oppressor are the minds of the oppressed. Women have been marginalized, disenfranchised at the hands of misogynistic mindsets and thinking

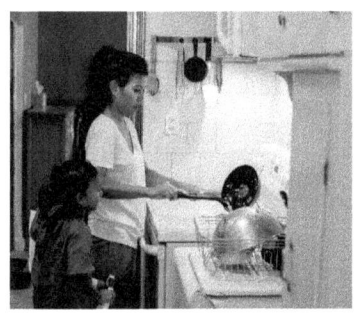

for thousands of years. Don't look for a chapter that's titled evolution of the 21st century man because it hasn't changed for centuries. Many women never realized that all of the jewels on the crown of humanity was already in their possession. For thousands of years, women were raised and taught that a woman's place was in the home. Women have grown through education and evolved in our political landscape one inch at a time. Women rediscovered what they already knew, that they have been bamboozled over the last 500 years and beyond. Men were given tremendous credit for satisfying primary domestic needs which consisted of (water, food, shelter, and clothing) As the old-timers would say "someone to bring home the bacon" or "a man with some benefits". The average woman was socially conditioned to a domestic role that lacked congruence. Women grew the family by having an average of 4 children or more for most of the 1900s. In fact, it was not uncommon to hear someone say that they have 8 biological brothers and sisters. As propagation shifted in high gear, the average household was approximately 6 or more including the adults. Henry Ford had already sold over 8 million cars before the 19th amendment was signed and ratified in the year 1919 giving women the right to vote. The anti-slavery movement propelled women out of the house-hold and church and into politics to advocate for their rights. Black women for most of the deep south had to wait even longer as a result of the denial of voter registrations, poll tax, and barred from ballot boxes etc. It was not until 1965 that black women were allowed to vote without any resistance with the passing of the voters' right act. Many women sacrificed and placed their own personal dreams and aspirations on the perimeter of their domestic life to facilitate the primary needs of family. Most women took on full time positions managing domestic activity that consist of raising their family, cooking, cleaning, homework and managing the roll of psychiatrist, psychologist, economist, tutor, nurse, etc. These are some of the internal domestic responsibilities that one takes on when raising, nurturing children, and establishing effective domestic culture. At this time in history September 1, 1939, Hitler invaded Poland and Japan invaded China. This global destabilization essentially caused the US to start ramping up its arm forces. On the 16th of September 1940, the United States instituted the Selective Training and Service Act that required all men between the ages of 21 and 45 to register for the draft. The failure to register would get you a free ticket for room and board to club Fed. Something happened suddenly that caused the domestic "Richter scale" to move significantly. Japan bombed Pearl Harbor, Hawaii Dec 7, 1941. This forced the US into world war II the very next day. Most US families were affected because not only did we have to assist with fighting Hitler and Germany but we simultaneously had to fight Japan. This forced most able body men between the ages of 21 and 45 men out of the house and into the war for over the next 4 years. The actual number of men registered was 50 million and approximately 10 million were inducted. The US had no other choice because Japan and Germany were getting out of control. If we did nothing, I assure all of you that you would be speaking German or Japanese right about now. Women were recruited to work in the factories that their men vacated to assist with manufacturing, ammunition, weapons, planes, and ships. Women for the first time in modern history got a real taste of becoming a significant income earner out of necessity. The war ended after the US dropped bombs on Hiroshima and Nagasaki in 1945, which effectively caused Japan to capitulate. After the smoke cleared, 291,000 men never made it back home. After the war, capitalism shifted in high gear and the need for the working class grew rapidly. This was the birth of what we now call the (baby boomers). There was such a national fear of a potential world war III, that couples began to accelerate propagation exponentially on the fear that their families would be annihilated in a nuclear disaster. This time frame was significant because it's the first time that women entered the workforce in mass numbers. I want to stop you for one moment and I want to go to your streaming service and look up one of my long-time favorite movies with Richard Geer's title "An Officer and A Gentleman". Richard Geer is a naval aviator and a young lady who works in the textile industry falls in love with him. Her desire has always been to start a family with a serviceman. The criteria for many women during that era was someone who was loving and financially stable with good health benefits. It did not hurt if he was handsome also. As women began to earn more income and increase education, their voices got louder and stronger. If you own a home that was built before 1970 chances are that it was built with a 7' long closet in the owner's suite. One side for him and the other for her. Small bathroom and a small but functional kitchen. As women's income became more competitive, builders had to change house designs to accommodate the needs of the professional woman. Massive walk-in closets, sunken tubs, dual vanity, gourmet kitchen, etc. In fact, I told my wife that I projected that within the next 10 years we will have globally the highest percentage of single 50-year-old women in recent history. She said what is your reasoning. As women's education and income increased over the last 100 years, the need for a man's income became less relevant. I said, "men and women seek money for different reasons honey". Women seek money for comfort so that they gain certainty. Men seek money for power so that they can gain control. Women's careers eventually took precedence over building a family. The women I interviewed seem to have a consensus with regards to having a mate whose income and education are congruent or greater than their own for the sake of greater financial comfort and intellectual sparing. The difference between the 21st century woman, the 19th and 20th century woman, as it relates to income synergy, is that the 19th century and 2/3 of the 20th century woman were, in most cases, completely dependent upon their mates' income to satisfy primary domestic needs. The 21st century woman knows that, with a little sacrifice and adjustment, she can still travel the world, open businesses, run companies and own their own home without anyone's support. I believe that the average professional woman looks at a man's income today as more of a relationship perk rather than a necessity. A lot like getting travel miles on your credit card. As a result, today's woman does not have to settle for inadequacies or reduce their standards to fit within the parameters of interesting prospects the way that women of the past did. This societal curse of women's rights has proliferated for so long that many men still don't realize that their grandfathers' relationship template has fallen into a dark empty cavern and stamped with the word obsolete. The reason I speak so much about women in this chapter is because women have spent a century making radical and progressive changes while most men were still asleep. Most men dominated households began to transition to more balance households in the mid-60s with the introduction of the Gen "X". In 1960, a woman made 61 cents compared to every dollar that a man made. I know of several guys my age when we were young that were fully aware of their father's infidelity. As a child, I would hear chatter asking the question why won't she just leave. Most women did not leave because once they made an economic evaluation, they took the path that they felt would not interrupt the existing lifestyle. In 2019, a woman earns 80 Cents to every dollar her male counterpart earned according to a recent census report. Another study by the institute for women policy research estimates that women won't completely close the gap until 2059. Since 1917 over 365 women have served in congress, senate and delegates. Women currently represent 20% of all mayors in the country and 30% of the municipal council positions. I want you to quickly reference a study conducted by the power research center below. Professional / Ph.D. Women between the ages of 40-44 with children were 34% in the early 90s compared to 23% in 2008.

As women take on more professional and career-oriented positions in the workforce, the desire to raise a family becomes secondary and as a result, are more likely to have fewer children. Here is a quick story, I was watching an interview with Charles Schwab, for those of you who are unaware who he is, his company ranked number two for investment bankers in the country. I'm amazed by the fact that he is still living quite healthy and astute. He was very candid during his interview which I respect so much. He talked about the struggles economically when he was young and the fact that he had suffered from dyslexia like Einstein. He said his regrets were centered around the fact that he wished he spent more time with his kids when they were younger. He said he worked late hours almost everyday building his brokerage. He paused and said that today he probably would not be considered to be a great dad. Here is a self-made billionaire acknowledging that his role as a husband would be slightly different today in comparison to the way it was in the 50s. During that time frame of the 50s and 60s, his primary role was to be a leader and a provider. What I respect about his comment is the fact that he recognizes and made midlife adjustments. Many baby boomer fathers operated off of one rule and that was the golden rule. "He who had the gold got to rule" he could only teach what he knew how to do and that was work and control. Let me be clear, this is not a generalized indictment against all men of the past, but I believe that it certainly is a significant number. The 21st-century man is trying to make adjustments in mid-flight with low fuel. He is just realizing that his income alone can no longer yield him the level of relevance that his father and grandfather once had. The 21st century man has to modify and resynchronize his relationship template if he wants to establish greater relevance in today's relationships. Many of us spend too much time concerned about what we are not getting out of a relationship and less time spent on what's being deposited. A good friend of mine told me that his wife shut down on him months ago. For those of you who don't know, that's a man's code word for "no sex". I said, "look man, I'm not a counselor but I speak based on experience and I have compiled about 20 years of research in an effort to improve myself". "When was the last time you looked your wife in the eyes with the same intensity that you did when you first dated?" I told him, "how much do you appreciate her existence and the fine job she has done with nurturing and providing for your kids with the skills that you lack?" When was the last time you guys held hands and walked through a park with your cell phones off? When was the last time that you guys went out dancing passionately in the middle of the dance floor at a local hot spot? Have you taken your wife to a 5-star restaurant lately or even brought her some flowers on a non-holiday? His answer to all of my questions was "no". I said, "I just did all of those things over the past 8 weeks". I said, "look, your problem is that you spend your time concerned about being short-changed and I spend my time giving the change". Look I don't have a perfect relationship. Just the other day my wife and I were in the car and I became so irritated because sometimes I feel like I'm on a driver's test. Stop here! Watch that car! There is a parking space over there! It irritated me so much that I had thoughts of getting out of the car and walking home. I told him that his concerns are not that much different than mine. Where we differ is that I honor and promote my wife daily. My wife never has to ponder a dubious thought on whether or not I love her. What we do for another person will always demonstrate twice as much as what we say. You spend your days dwelling on what you are not getting and I ponder how can I give more that is non-contingent on what she does for me. See this is the fundamental difference in the principles of reciprocity and quid quo pro. He says, "Edward, why you have to get so damn technical?" I said, "life is technical". I said, "quid pro quo, derived from Latin, means an exchange for services just like bartering". It means what I do for you is contingent upon what you do for me. One hand washes the other. I operate off the universal laws of reciprocity. I told him that my wife is not the reservoir of my spiritual deposits, she is the beneficiary. I just reached a point in my life where I became exhausted by operating from this social measuring stick of "what did you do for me?" What I do for my wife is non-contingent upon what she does for me. I care, but I can't be overly concerned about it. I know some may feel that this is a bit out there, but when my mind got more in tune with nature and its protocols, my relationship got better. You can never win by trying to quantify what someone does for you. Life will make the corrections for you. If you give the world a dollar of effort, unfortunately, you will receive about a dollar in return. When growing up my father worked and fixed everything in the home. Even it wasn't right, it was going to work when he got finished. He would make me repair my car, change my flat tire, build my wooden go-cart and so on. We had pliers and screwdrivers in our hands at age 7. Those days, I feel were the best days of my life because they taught me how to be self-sufficient. 4 years of college didn't come close to those experiences. I was cutting grass around our pool one day and ran over a hive of yellow jackets in the ground that did not want me near them. Apparently, they became irritated and proceeded to sting me multiple times. I had just treated the pool with a high dose of chlorine, so taking a dive after the stings was not a healthy option. I went into the house not realizing that my wife was in the window having a thrill at how fast I ran across the yard. When I went into the kitchen to get some water, she started to kiss me passionately over the sink. I asked what that was for and she said, "it turns me on when I see you work in the yard". I said, "well let me go and do some more work". "I think I will cut the grass again because I missed some spots", I said jokingly. She smiled and said, "you always make me feel secure". Remember that most of our self-esteem is developed before age 7. As women's needs and desires shifted, the baby-boomers, that men defined as those born between (1946 and 1964), were so concerned about not having their offspring working as hard as they did, that they forgot to pass down the ruggedness, grit, and work ethics that built their characters. 30 years later, we have a vast number of men who can navigate through a video game but can't change their car tires. The results are in and many parents have participated in failed parenting experiments and strategies that have left many of our young men stripped of critical thinking skills. Although, App developments are beneficial, it has exacerbated the need for self-innovation and creativity. A growing number of men are becoming metro-sexualized to the point that their nails are more important than cutting their grass or changing an outlet in their home. It's not about whether you have the money to get someone to do it, it's about developing alternative skill sets before an adversity exposes itself. Here is a quick story, a married female friend of the family had a leaky toilet, I told her that she can get a new tank kit from home depot for less than $15. After she purchased, she was experiencing difficulty installing it while her husband was busy watching movies. She faced timed me and I assisted in giving her instructions for her to finish the process, Sadly, men can no longer use the fact that these life skills were not passed down to them. I can pay to have most of the things done around the home, but I choose to do many household chores because I take pride in the process. I aim to demonstrate to my wife that if my money suddenly dries up, I will

RECIPROCITY

always be able to offer you certainty. I told her that I will never in life let another person's decision dictate how and when we eat. The recession of 2008 created very stressful times for most Americans, especially those who were in business. The banking system was on the verge of a complete financial collapse because of the wall street led greed. They had a great time selling toxic mortgages to the secondary money markets and giving real estate loans to people who did not qualify under normal criteria, were packaged as securities and sold on wall street. When homeowners could no longer pay the system, it became over-leveraged and as a result, led to the closure of major banking institutions. My real estate office dwindled from 250 agents to 10 in 6 months, with many of my agents shifted to w-2 positions to secure income. I remember telling my wife during that time that the utility room was flooding because the Hot water heater was faulty. Money was tight and she asked me what we were going to do? I told her to get into the car and head to Home Depot. We purchased a Hot water heater. The box was too large to place in the back of the car, so we took it out the box at home depot parking lot and slid it in the back seat. We went home and disconnected the other heater. She asked me if I've ever installed a Hot water heater? I said no, but I have something that my parents gave me a long time ago and that's called confidence and common sense. Two hours later, after watching a couple of YouTube videos, we were taking hot showers again. I share this story because adversity has a very interesting way of revealing one's character. Women, on the other hand, have to be careful not to be too indulged in things that you may be able to do and try to leave somethings for them to do as well. I think it's important to defer or punt (as we say in football), so that your husband or mate has the opportunity to get acknowledgement and establish masculine value. I'm not suggesting that you can't do it, but let's be realistic, He makes 100k and so do you. If you are not careful, your decision to leave nothing for him to do could throw off polarity. I will get into more of that in the next chapter. If you are one of my male readers please don't feel as if this is a book that condemns men, because it's not. Before I offer solutions, I must first identify the problems. I know of several women who choose to share a good man part-time, rather than have a bad man full-time. This behavior demonstrates that there is a thirst for quality men whose masculinity is not threatened by equality. The 21st century woman will have to be patient because this is going to take a while. Men who refuse to capitulate to the new order often pursue less-educated women whose needs tend to be more traditional and economic based. The problem with this arrangement, provided he is an educated man, is the fact that his cerebral growth is often impeded because he does not get a steady dose of intellectual sparing which allows him to grow. Most men are often wired to take the less-restrictive path that satisfies their sexual needs. This monetary positioning allows the economic flexing to maintain the desired control level that they often find appealing. My wife has 7 girlfriends in their early 40's. All single and have corporate positions with earnings over 100K. This is evident and represents my commentary in this chapter. My speculation because I realize that I do not have all the answers, is the fact that many women will have to become teachers of new love covenants and if they are not willing to adapt you, move on and don't capitulate because being single is a social status, not a character status. Oftentimes, this is a very arduous process because most hormonal exchanges, which I identified later in the book, have already taken place. Feelings in the form of lust and infatuation can often intensify during the incipient stages of dating which causes

hard questions and decisions to be more challenging. This increases the chance of compromise, which is unacceptable, as it relates to the new love order. That would be taking a step backwards more like placing a drop of oil on a squeaky wheel. Unfortunately, professional women today are going to have to sit down and make an attempt with

RECIPROCITY

their partners and teach them what's important. This book would be a good start. Not because I wrote it, but rather this is one of the primary reasons I wrote it. Most men are still operating off old relationship covenants. The fact that we don't like to read relationship books or get instructions from them often exacerbates this challenge. I love it when my wife has a better income month than I do, because I get to spend more time in the park running with our son. Personally, I believe that when we assess the true value of a women's presence her income exceeds what a man earns based on her value to society. Another quick story, I managed over 270-real estate agents at one point, so you can imagine how large our sales meetings were. I often provided food and refreshments to incentivize the unmotivated. I would set a budget of about $1000. I would sometimes assist with preparing and transforming our flex space into a more buffet-style setting. I placed a table cloth, a punch bowl, a pile of napkins, forks, and spoons on the table and felt I did a good job. My office manager, a female, came into the room, she paused and smiled. Then she asked me to go sign some checks, to get me out of the room. When the meeting started, I came back with my bullet points for my speech and the damn room looked like we were dining on the roof top of a 5-star hotel. I am not exaggerating, there is no way in hell I would have been able to see that far. The primary function of masculine energy is to condense life, so that it can gain control. One other hand, feminine energy is predisposed to augment life so that it has flavor and excitement. Take a break now and go to YouTube search videos of rams banging each other with their horns for hours. Have you ever wondered why? It is because sheep or ewes are typically attracted to the rams that gives them the most certainty, comfort and trust. If you placed all the women on another planet, men would quit their jobs the next day, well maybe not the next day but certainly after they get their last check because there would be no incentive to continue, no one to impress. Most men spend their life trying to appeal to women because they know who holds all the cards. The 21st century man has hard choices and decisions to make if he wants to maintain relevance in today's relationship. Over the last 100 years, the 21st century professional women has completely revised and amended their entire relationship manual and most men are just getting their copy. The title is called "paradigm shift".

Laws of Polarity

One of my favorite subjects is relationship polarity. Before I get started, you will often hear me speak of feminine energy and masculine energy. The reason I have to differentiate between the two is because the energies have nothing to do with gender. I have to disclose this out of respect for the (LGBTQ) community. I believe that polarity lies at the epicenter of laws of attraction. Everything in nature requires balance. If nature did not have a balance the world could not survive including our relationships. For example, the sun never burns out because of the process of nuclear fusion. This occurs because the helium feeds off the hydrogen and the hydrogen feed off the helium. This synergistic relationship is both relevant and necessary for maximum efficiency. This does not mean that two people who are wired to be extremely detailed oriented, work positions at NASA on formulas for the space shuttle can't get along. It just means that they have to work harder on maintaining lust and spontaneous actions. Under Doctor Robert Rhome's personality profile, which I have studied and taught much of his teachings to over 200 persons in my real estate classes over the last 15 years, We would call them "C" personalities. In other words, they may even write on a note pad as to whose turn it is to initiate sex that night. That relationship's juice, fire, and excitement may be a challenge. The antithesis of this arrangement is two people who are extremely people-oriented. We call them "I" personalities. For Instance, one may work in sales and the other is a musician. The problem with this arrangement is that life is so exciting that they might even forget to pay the electric bill because there are no structures and the smallest things get overlooked. You never have to worry about where an "I" personality is in a room because they are always talking. Everything in life for this couple is a dance. I walked in a married couple's home, married for less than a year and the energy was so low that it felt like a funeral home. I assure you that are likely "C" or "S" personalities. I know several couples like this, if you give me a day, I can predict what they are doing. This is a problem because dopamine responds to novelty, rewards, and unpredictable events. They could stay married for 40 years but their lives tend to be so predictable and structured to the point it lacks excitement, fire, and juice. Let me give you another example. Have you ever seen a really attractive woman when she is out on the town? She is beautiful, successful, educated and the guy that she is with is tattooed from rooter to the tooter unshaven and in need of a barber. You notice that he is leading her by holding her hand as they maneuver in the crowd. You say to yourself wow! what is that beautiful, stunning, and jovial woman doing with him? One of her interest could be because she can't control him. That becomes an attraction in and of itself. His radical idealisms let her know that he could care less about what someone thinks. The relationship may not have a great shelf life, but for a few months or so she finds it satisfying. Regardless of what you may think, she gets satisfaction based on the fact that her feminine energy is pre-wired to seek comfort and certainty. Maximum polarity exists because this gentleman regardless of his external disposition exudes high levels of masculine energy and confidence. Sex is probably exciting for her as well as a result of maximum polarity. This is the primary reason of the old phrase "nice guys come in last". The nice guy in this particular example means well but the reason he never got the date is because his energy although nice and respectful does not offer adequate levels of direction and certainty to satisfy her thirst for security and certainty. Recently, my son met a very nice young lady and he came to me for some advice on where to take her to on a date. I said you must understand that really outgoing women really love a man that knows what he wants, has vision, direction, smart, and has a bit of a swagger. Why don't you call her? And when you do, please don't ask her "what would she like to do?" This would be a turn off and give an indication that you are indecisive. Ask for her availability and let her know that you are coming to pick her up. Look very nice and wear some jeans. Please don't take her to dinner or a restaurant, she's done that about 50 times already. I told him to take her to Shenandoah mountains, which was about one hour drive. Also, I suggested that they should go horse-riding in the mountains and then take her to lunch. I suggested that they should drive for 5 miles and go on a tour in the caverns. He took my advice and called me in about a week or so, and said, "dad, she mentioned that it was the best date she has ever been on". I replied and said, "see, where you take a woman gives her an indication of how you feel about her and reveals a little bit about you character". Recently, I saw a very happy female couple walking in the park when I went for my morning run. The fact that they both are female is irrelevant. Polarity must still exist for a sustainable shelf life. One of the women was dressed in a beautiful spring dress and the other had a baseball jersey, jeans, and a baseball cap turned around backwards. Their relationship works because it's balanced. Most really feminine women will tell you that it drives them crazy to be in the presence of a man who complies to everything they ask. Here's a quick story, my wife confessed to me 8 years after we decided to be exclusive. She said, "honey, you know that if I could control you, I could not be with you". The feminine energy is always testing to make sure that its life's parameters are safe and secure. Deep down, it knows that if you capitulate and acquiesce to everything they ask, then you are not masculine enough to offer the certainty that they desire. I remember a point in time when we lived in the forest with the animals, and as a young adult, I thought women wanted nice guys who were ambitious, compliant, smart, spiritual, and an overall complete gentleman. The reality is that they do, but there has to be a balance that is capable of exuding a level certainty and swagger, otherwise the polarity gets thrown off course. I did not figure out this maze until I was in my 30s. Unfortunately, the feminine energy will sometimes ask masculine energy to do things that it's really not interested in doing. The question becomes, why did you ask it in the first place? Most women, who are feminine energy dominant, don't really know themselves. My wife, without question, is the antithesis of who I am, which is why the fire and juice remains at optimum levels. One moment she is talking to me, 5 minutes later she is talking about episodes of her favorite shows with her girlfriend and then in the same breath ask me to make a special run to the store. I must admit that it comes at me so fast that I get dizzy and have to sit down. One day, I walked in the door and I sensed she was having a moment, that was my cue to quickly get out of here because I'm about to get rained on without an umbrella. At that moment, I understood that she does not need me to talk, but just listen to her. Over the years, I have grown not to take it personal anymore. The feminine energy is a storm of emotions, and as a result some days, the weather patterns may not line up properly and you end up with a thunderstorm. **When a storm is approaching, if you do nothing, the sun always returns.** I have come to realize that the feminine energy is not meant to be understood it just has to be managed. I authored a class titled "The psychology of real estate", where I taught to over 250 people. Oftentimes, I spoke about emotional management and how our perceptions have direct impacts on our realities. This is the case even on a cellular level as it relates to false activation of the sympathetic nervous system and how it influences cortisol levels unnecessarily. I will dive deeper into that in the chapter "Physiology of Emotions." In other words, I am extremely mal-tempered because I have learned over the years to qualify those with who I argue. Everyone is not worthy of my argument. In life, one thing that we can never make up for is our time. Therefore, why give it to someone that doesn't matter. I'm speaking specifically as it relates to arguments that don't register on my Richter scale. Another quick story, in 12 years of being in a relationship with my wife, I have never made debasing comments to her that could be categorized as verbally abusive. I have come out of character as a result of contentious matters that have surfaced on a couple of occasions over the years. Without going into detail, I had a few choice words one evening over something that I thought was rather trivial. After my apologies did not work things became elevated to the point that I became louder. She knows that this tone for me is not common. She started to laugh and I thought something was wrong until she hugged, kissed me passionately, and said, "I love to see you get angry from time to time". My interpretation is that she did not orchestrate or premeditate this event, there was a legitimate concern about something I had done that she was not in agreement with. Let's rewind and venture a few thousand years ago, when we lived in the forest and jungles with the rest of the animals. My theory is that, our creator like every other animal, has possibly predisposed us to prune and weed out the weak by design because it was necessary to have the fittest physically and mentally to protect the offspring. Some men call it domesticated bitching, I call it domesticated testing. Let's take a brief look at conception. The average healthy man discharges, during an orgasmic event, approximately 300-400 million sperm and 99.9 percent never make it to the fallopian tubes. Everything in life is wired to weed out the weak and I believe that we are no different. Let me make this clear before I get nasty emails. I am not insinuating that a woman is incapable of being self-sufficient and protecting her own nest. The purpose of a union is to love and share responsibilities through reciprocal delegation. Here is a funny story. I was quarterbacking in a football game and one of my offensive linemen was blocking like a matador. I told him, "if you are not going to block the other guy and give your best effort, I would prefer that you not be here". That way I know what side to run to. When you pretend to block it exposes me to injury. Feminine energy expects you to block and when you are operating under false pretenses it could make you expendable. One night while asleep, my wife heard a noise in the basement. She kicked me in the shin and said, "I heard something", that's code word for "get the hell up and go see what's going on". I told her to stay here and listen closely and if you hear things escalating, call the police. Men would never lose the opportunity to get an acknowledgement for performing a good task. I went in the basement and noticed that the wind was causing the back door to rattle a bit. Once I secured the door, the noise went away. When feminine energy senses that masculine energy is incapable of fighting for what it believes by consistently capitulating to all resistance, this can cause polarity to slowly dissipate if it becomes chronic. There are times when I'm not in the mood to fight. When you get the chance, I would like you to pull the map and look up the Gulf of Mexico. A couple of years ago, I took my family on a vacation to south of Tampa and was surprised by how warm and calm the water was. I want you to use your imagination for the sake of my point. View the water as representing feminine energy not a female or male. I want you to view its shores as masculine energy. The gulf, with just a little change in wind speed, looks like you are in the middle of the ocean and has the capacity to sink a large ship. This is the basis of feminine energy. Feminine energy is always testing the shoreline's integrity. If it does not respect its shores it will take over like a tsunami. The feminine energy is wired to augment everything in life to give it substance and energy. Masculine energy seeks to reduce and simplify life so that it can establish parameters. The feminine energy is the most beautiful thing in the world. I would estimate based on my research, 80 percent of women are wired by default as being feminine energy dominant. On the other hand, 20 percent is masculine energy dominant. The masculine energy dominant woman is wired to take control, she is often passionate about entrepreneurship, political leadership, CEO of company, coach, team captain, and so on. This energy is more likely to attract the 20 percent of men who are feminine energy dominant. You can give a feminine energy woman bag of groceries and they will make it into a fabulous dinner with a table cloth and candles. You can give them an empty house with no furniture and they will make it into a beautiful home. You can give them a seed of a man and they will give you a beautiful family. The feminine energy, as far as I'm concern, is what dominates the world. Masculine energy by default, looks to take big things and make it small. Masculine energy is about simplicity, problem solving direction and control. This is why it does not like asking for directions. Masculine energy has to take advantage of all the acknowledgement points it can muster in a day. Masculine energy wakes up looking for opportunity to ask a smiling woman. "Can I get the door for you?". "Would you like me to help you clean your car?", "Can I take you to dinner", "help you with your grass?" Anything that it can find to accumulate acknowledgement credit. If you don't believe me try this test. Ladies, the next time you are in a room full of associates, pretend that you have something that is broken or not working properly and I want you to say "does anyone know what is going on with this?" Everyone who is masculine energy dominant will probably rise up and almost compete for the opportunity to offer solutions. Masculine energy responds to challenges and feminine energy responds to love, affection, attention, and praise. Challenges are opportunities to gain acknowledgement which is later exchanged for social pleasures. Acknowledgement is a form of a man's sexual currency. What masculine energy must understand is that you will never get the beauty of all of the gifts that feminine energy has to offer, if it does not have certainty. Certainty is the code word for trust. Feminine energy is about freedom and being alive. Now before I go further, let me elaborate on this point because I don't want to get a bunch of nasty emails. My wife does not expect me to control her, but she does expect me to resolve the issues and concerns in which she either has no interest or feel is more appropriate for my skill set. Feminine energy is always testing and evaluating the shoreline integrity. If you ever get the opportunity to visit a heard of sheep during mating season. I want you to get out your camera and ask yourself, "why are the rams (Male Sheep) ramming each other in the head violently for hours?" Well, they are fighting for male dominance. They know that their skills are being evaluated by hundreds of sheep (ewes). The sheep makes assessments on the strongest ram in which it will grant sexual access to grow its family as a result of certainty. This is not just sheep, it's true for just about every animal in nature. I was watching an animal show on lions in the Serengeti in Africa. A study was conducted years ago at Bern University in Switzerland to determine if opposites attract on a cellular (DNA) level. They collected DNA of 49 females and 44 males' students. They asked the men to wear cotton tee-shirts free of fragrance and perfumes for a couple of days. Once complete, they were given individual plastic bags to place the shirts in after the 2 days. I'm condensing the study a bit so that I don't bore you with too many details. The women were told to smell each bag. The study concluded that the MHC genes in the women gravitated to the men whose MHC genes were most opposite of their own. Scientists believe that this could be possible because the body may be wired to seek opposites, to possibly optimize immune function with bacterium that they did not possess in their gut and for overall protection of offspring. We seek in others what we lack in ourselves. I remember hearing older couples in the 80s usually says things like, opposites attract and never gave it any thought. In fact, I thought it was part of some old folk saying until I started to study psychology. With my real estate background, I have attended over 2000 settlements. I told a friend that I have never seen a couple where both husband and wife scrutinized the contract. One scrutinizes and the other typically just signs. I want you to reflect on your own family of different couples and you will notice that in most of the functional relationships, that polarity does exist. Remember, in order to have sexual attraction, the presence of predator and prey must exist for long-term sexual health. When your relationship gets to a place where your significant other knows everything you are going to do sexually, it is not the best to sustain long-term sexual health. Complacency can evolve to predictability, and predictability can cause hormonal deficits that ultimately effect arousal and climax. My wife could not begin to tell you what, where or how long sex will be most of the time. I get my wife flowers every Friday. I started about two years ago because I was beginning to feel that flowers and appreciation were being dictated by commercialized holidays. So I said, why can't every Friday be Valentine's Day. It evolved as I made self-assessments and the realignment and calibration of our conscious energy and vibrations. If I ever get a sense that complacency is setting in, I'm off and running to make adjustments. Most couples believe that the marital contract they sign committing their life to another person is enough to sustain great emotional health. All couples have a responsibility to make self-assessments on relationship performance weekly. At this point, I want to highlight this opinion. It is not my responsibility to manage what my wife does for me. However, it is my responsibility to manage and improve what I do to improve myself as a husband. I don't know about you, but life for me is much easier when I focus more on giving love rather than receiving it. My wife could curse at me on a Thursday and she is still getting flowers on Friday. Getting my wife flowers every Friday was never contingent upon what she does for me. This is my process and it can't be deviated. If the person in your life is mature and responsible changes, due to operating by the reciprocity laws and should show remarkable changes over time. There is a radical difference between feeling like you are a victim rather than a victor. I'm fortunate my wife responds by giving me more, so now I'm afraid to stop. A good friend of mine works in a medical center. He told me that a very successful and attractive female doctor friend asked him where all the good men were. She has never been engaged or married. Let me go on record and say that there is absolutely nothing wrong with living your life basking in your singleness. In fact, I suggest that you date yourself before entering a relationship. It allows you to self-reflect and identifies your primary needs and desires. I have many business associates who are in their 40s and 50s who have never been married or engaged. This woman desires to have a life partner and is having difficulty in making a connection. He said, he remembers her from college and indicated that she was a cheerleader for the football team. He described her as being very jovial, gregarious, fun-loving, and free-spirited. She is now in her late 40's single and very accomplished. She travels the world; she keeps adequate savings and has great credit. He asked me the question and said, "Ed why do you think that she is having so much difficulty in finding someone to spend significant time with?" I felt compelled to offer input on the subject and rendered an opinion of a few possibilities. I said, "Thomas, you have to understand that we are literally in a social paradigm shift between man and women". He told me to expound on my point. I replied, "For the first time in modern history, man and woman are on the same parallel as far as education and income". The dynamics of our domestic lives have shifted considerably in the last 100 years. Good women are challenged on whether they should lower the bar and reduce their relationship criteria and standards to accommodate the inadequacies in men who are oblivious to what changes have transpired in the last 100 years. Good masculine men who have good-paying blue-collar positions are often overlooked by single 40-year-old college-educated women because they believe that their degree is more important than his electrician license. Most men rely on relationship skills that have proliferated from 1000 years of male-dominated control. Baby boomer and earlier dads often told their children that I'm going to make it so that you don't have to work as hard, not realizing that this was a very significant attribute that gave them their work ethic and character. The 21st century women are taking auditions for men who can assist them in going to places where they have never been to mentally. The men who will tear and rip all forms of fear from their heart and replace them with support and certainty. The men who inundates her on a daily basis with love, affection, attention, and praise. She is looking for a guy who has plans to circumnavigate the globe for new opportunities and exposure. One who operates with a swagger that has direction and purpose. She is looking for that man who understands the female anatomy and is capable of taking her on a perpetual adventure sexually that has no beginning and has no end. Most of all, masculine energy must understand that the feminine energy does not just want love, affection, attention, and praise, it requires those in the same way that a plant requires sunlight. The cars, houses, dates gifts, and trips are no longer sufficient enough to sustain 21st century relationships beyond the novelty stages with the professional women. I said, "Thomas, what's the difference between a dinosaur and a cockroach?" His response was the difference in size. I said, "you get one damn point for trying". I told him that the difference between the dinosaur and the cockroach was adaptation. The cockroach is still around today because it adapted to a changing environment and the dinosaur did not. I said, "look Thomas, she was probably born based on the info provided as a very feminine girl, who played with dolls and helped mommy bake cookies in the oven". She loved to go shopping and overall had a very gregarious disposition. She went to college for 8 years to become a doctor and evolved to having a very successful career as a medical doctor. Masculine energy is required to run business, supervise, leadership, coaching, CEO, COO, CFO, and so on. Masculine energy is not always attractive but it's powerful. Masculine energy gives direction, guidance, leadership, and structure. We all have some level of masculine energy, some more than others. From what we know, this doctor's energy core is feminine based, in other words, she is wired as being feminine energy dominant. This means that the relationship stars alignment desires the antithesis of her core. The problem is she socially functions in her daily life with masculine armor. She operates in a restricted space that has been conditioned based on past experiences. Let me elaborate, our experiences generate references, our references have a direct impact on behavior, and behavior influences decisions. The decision is the father of our actions. After you date so many times the mind subconsciously believes that the world has nothing to offer you. She has suppressed her natural free-flowing gregarious personality, forgot how to smile to reveal her core energy. We so often get caught up in our careers and chasing money that we forget how to smile and laugh. Masculine men run away from women who exude high levels of masculine energy because it's just like hanging out with the guys. The danger with this armor is that she is more likely to attract someone who has a poor shelf life because she is not operating from her core. Most men wake up looking for a smiling woman that is confident in herself and in her abilities. Someone asked me years ago, where are all the good men? I responded not at the bar you just came from. We come together because we have something in common but we get together because we have polarity. I asked what are your interests? She said technology sales. Why are you not attending tech conferences in Las Vegas, technology association of America, nonprofit organizations? What type of guy spends his Saturday afternoon cleaning the riverbanks for the sake of the planet? What type of guy spends a couple of weeks in a year volunteering for an organization to feed the homeless? Does the word "selfless" ring a bell? My wife personifies feminine energy. She gives our home sunshine and life. She is in business, but she is masterful in turning off her masculine energy when coming home for the sake of maintaining what I call "domestic polarity". I can hear her coming through the door singing her favorite song. She throws my son's foam basketball at my head when I'm trying to get some work done. She dances sexy in front of me trying to get my attention. One night while I was typing a contract, I told her that I will not be coming to bed at my normal time because I was busy with work. She later came into the office with a tee-shirt, wearing nothing else, and told me goodnight. As I lift my head and watched her walk out of the door, I suddenly discovered that I have the time to go to bed now and I will complete the contract in the morning. I closed my laptop so fast that I damaged my keyboard. More of that later in the chapter "physiology of attraction". I often say that if your market does not offer quality prospects then maybe you need to change your market. In other words, you are not going to find gold nuggets in a sports bar. Women have to be cognizant of the fact that they don't to overindulge in many of the household chores that men look forward to completing. If your salary is equal then some men start to feel inadequate. If he comes home and you have hung three pieces of drywall in the basement, cut the grass, and took out the trash, inadequacy sets in. Here is quick story, I was visiting my brother who recently purchased a very large colonial. The basement was unfinished and we were discussing the layout and piping for the bathroom for the contractor. His wife arrived home and came downstairs kissed him on the cheek and went back up the stairs. It was quite obvious that the level of trust in his decision-making, as it related to finishing the basement, was well established. She did not come downstairs asking the contractor questions or getting involved in where the door was going to be. This is important because I have seen couples argue over the simplest things after buying a new home. She obviously punted this task because of her level of trust in him. Also, Women have to understand that approximately 20 percent of the men are feminine energy dominant. Let me reiterate that. I'm am not referring to a gay man as it relates to the 20 percent, although many in this number could be. This is the type of guy who loves to dance, loves to shop, he notices women's shoes and hairs, and so on. He may even get his nails done every Friday. He was also the captain of his high school basketball team. Life for him is always a dance. What he desires most is freedom. This type of guy desires a woman who makes almost all the financial decisions. That is, where they will live, what schools the kids attend, the family diet, and so on. What he will do is attend the PTA meeting while she is at work. He will spend time with the kids at the playground. He cooks, cleans, and establishes his relevance in other areas of concern. This is why a lot of your hardcore business women have such a reduced pool to choose from. Many musicians and artists are dominant with feminine energy. Feminine and masculine energy has nothing to do with gender. I know of a couple, every holiday season the wife assembles all the toys while her father comes over to cut their grass in the summer. In fact, her husband does nothing around the home that one would consider as being manly. The relationship survives because polarity exist. It works for them because everyone understands their roles. If the Doctor's base and core are truly feminine, she has to recognize that the energy that's needed for her business success has to be segregated if she is to attract a masculine man. Masculine men, by default, wake up looking for a woman who smiles. We gravitate to relationships that are the antithesis of who we are. I hear this all the time. I could not be prouder of the progress that women have made over the last 100 years. We have to realize that everything comes with a cost. As professional feminine women take on positions of authority and power, it's imperative that they realize that the masculine energy that they exude during the day has to be managed otherwise the relationship polarity that exists in their domestic lives could be significantly compromised. Some women are challenged with this daily conversion because the men in their lives are weak and inadequate. She has to make the daunting decision on whether this is an acute relationship malfunction or a chronic ailment. If it's chronic, then hard decisions will have to be made to maintain the level of intimacy necessary to sustain a loving household. When a core base masculine partner neglects the marital duties in which he is responsible for and does not give a feminine woman love, affection, attention, praise, and most of all certainty. Polarity will dissipate rapidly as she overcompensates to take on additional relationship task and responsibilities. This is very dangerous because it could lead to what I call "deficiency exposure". Deficiency exposure occurs when, subconsciously, an individual's core needs are not being met. A good friend of mine told me that his wife, "went off on him over a f----ing plate in the sink. I told him that the plate is a symptom and you are perceiving it as the problem. This is very important because, it is the start of what could lead to a precipitous decline in quality intimacy.

When the needs of our mates are being neglected, this often gets gravitated to, what I call, "level (1) adultery". Level one adultery is often accompanied by denial. Let me give you an example. You suddenly give attention to the co-worker that has been asking you to go to lunch for the last year. He always told you how good your hair looked. He bought you a card on your birthday. He noticed the unique design on your nails. One Monday morning he told you how good you smelled. These downloads into our subconscious provide dopamine surges whether you like it or not. These sweet gestures filled the gap of what you were not receiving in your (7) year marriage. One night you have a nasty fight with your husband and the totality of these sweet gestures from Bernard at work led you down a path of destruction. So, you decide to capitulate to the pressure because of your level of frustration in your domestic life. The lunch evolved to an early dinner and hundreds of texts and phone calls. This is what I consider Level (1) adultery. Most people have affairs primarily because needs are not being met. You convince yourself that it's just a friend but the dopamine surges have become so addictive that you can't stop yourself. Once the mind becomes chemically influenced, you lose control until it dries up. The next thing we have is a full-blown physical affair with emotional (level 2) and physical (level 3) attachment which is the worst of them all. To summarize this: Level (1) is inappropriate communication, Level (2) hormonal and neurotransmitter-based chemical dependency Level (3) Intimacy. Remember what I said earlier, relationships don't end because of the lack of love they end because of the lack of intimacy. Polarity must be present in order to have a spark. I have found that most of the feminine energy-based adultery has been emotionally based while masculine energy adultery is more physically based. I want to circle back to the accomplished doctor. I explained to him that most men are trying to navigate through the 21st century relationships by using their grandfather's relationship template, which consists of a one-page instruction and here they are: (1) Get a good paying job (2) Pay all

RECIPROCITY

the bills in the house (3) Provide food and shelter for the entire family. (4) Demand sex from your wife regardless of how she feels and go to sleep. I am not using this example as a generalized indictment against all men. My dad was not certainly that way. We must acknowledge that this behavior was quite prevalent for centuries. Women have to understand that they hold the keys to the vault of most of the stimulation of "dopamine" in most men. Statistically, the average man thinks about sex 19 times a day and they can't have it without them. Women must not panic and should not capitulate to inadequacies and stubbornness. For example, when you write an offer to purchase a home, you typically write an offer subject to a home inspection. After the home inspection, a buyer would typically say, "I Joan Johnson agree to remove the inspection contingency provided the seller repair or replace the following". What if we date for 4 months and present our inspection addendum before having sex? I think we would find out a lot about the other person before wasting valuable time hoping that someone will evolve into this image of the perfect mate. I know I'm getting off track here but understand that we did not get in this space overnight and we certainly won't get out overnight. It's going to take some time for men, in general, to make the necessary societal adjustments to reestablish value and not control. Women today are looking for a man that is capable of making decisions and controlling situations in which they have no interest. Good men are passed over because they just don't know what to do. Antiquated relationship templates were successful for him but not for her. Many women, prior to the 1940s, made choices in a man based on income and stability. This is what I call Level (1) needs. He was considered to be a good man from the surface. All he had to do was pay the bills and be consistent. Most men knew this. He primarily operated off the golden rule. "He who had the gold got to rule." It was nothing for the industrial man and women to get married and have 5 to 7 children. Today, that is almost unheard of in an educated household. I don't want to get off track because the question was, "why is this educated woman having difficulty with commitment?" I don't know her personally but what she has to understand are the laws of polarity.

The 21st century masculine energy's relationship template is a work in progress, so we have to be patient. Most men are oblivious of the primary needs of 21st century woman. Many believe that if he continues to make lots of money, buy more gifts, and houses, that acknowledgement will soon follow. His relationship manual was authored by his grandfather and passed down by his father. In some cases, there were no teachers. So, he treats his woman based on the things that he likes rather than what she wants. If you are a male reader, I want you to stop for a moment and pat yourself on the back for taking the time to educate yourself in personal development. I also want to you to post what I'm about to say on the dashboard of your car and on your bedroom wall. "LAAP". This stands for love, affection, attention, and praise. On a long term, she could care less about your car, the house, or about the trips. The feminine energy does not just want love, affection, attention, and praise, the feminine energy "requires" love, affection, attention, and praise. Stop trying to spend so much time trying to figure out why and just deliver. When you view life from the lens of a man you will never see what she sees. When you view life from the lens of the past, you will always be blind in your present. Remember that "change" is the barometer in which talent skill and accomplishments are always evaluated. Your failure to change from antiquated ideals and habits could ultimately lead to the demise of your relationship. Guys, I will be candid for a quick story of my own. My wife spent about 2 hours at the Dominican salon getting a blowout treatment. From there, she spent another 2 hours getting manicure and pedicure. She came home, walked up the stairs and I said, "hello honey, would you like to go out to get a bite to eat?" I later apologized, almost with a tear in my eye, because I neglected level (2) need. Through my lens, it was not important but through hers it was everything. She needed me to let her know how beautiful she looked. The silkiness in her hair, how pretty and unique the design was on her nails. You may feel that it's insignificant through the eyes of a male but for her to be unnoticed by the man in her life was deflating. I never made that mistake again.

The Octopus Man

One morning, while driving our daughter to her freshman year at St. John's University in New York. We were ambivalent about the trip but knew that this has always been the primary goal in our domestic education. I felt compelled to give her some relationship advice since we knew that the sharks would be certainly roaming on campus and relationships will inevitably develop. I asked her if she was familiar with the octopus. She knew what it was, but just unfamiliar with its capabilities. I said that an octopus is one of three sea creatures in the world that fall under the category of "Cephalopod". She said dad, "come on, it's not that serious". I said, "yes, it is, let me tell you why". The reason why I used the Octopus to represent my point is because, the octopus is capable of not only changing its colors, it can also change its texture as well. If it needs to feel like coral and look like coral, it can. If it needs to look like sea weed and feel like sea weed, it can. If it needs to look like the sand and feel like the sand, it can. This is both used as a defense and an offense for its survival. I said, "look here, you are going to meet guys who are capable of changing their color and texture to represent what they think you may be looking for in a man. It's a very difficult process to weed out, so you have to be careful". The male version of the octopus falls under a specie of man called "womanizers". Womanizers often come from families in which love may not have adequately permeated the atmosphere and as a result have grown not to trust the process. In other words, they often view relationships as incarceration. Womanizers are often articulate, smart, gregarious, affectionate, and offer great fun times. They typically have one motive in mind, and that's to make themselves look and feel like the person you want them to be until he purges you of all your love and resources, much like a parasite. From the beginning, he never had any intent to be in the race long term. His job is to make you believe that his presence will yield you an abundance of love and prosperity. Now, my daughter, who was in the back seat getting and irritated because she can't listen to her playlist on her phone, started to listen and ask me questions. She asked, "how am I supposed to know if the good guys look just like the bad ones?" I said, "I don't have all the answers but one thing I can tell you for sure is that womanizers are sprinters. They operate like a cheetah on the African Serengeti". "If a cheetah can't catch its prey in 23 seconds they have to call off the chase or their bodies will over heat from exhaustion because of the high speeds". I said, "womanizers don't have enough resources and chicanery in their arsenal to last more than six months". A lot of their lies will start to unravel if you just wait. Mark twain said, "A LIE CAN TRAVEL A HALF WAY AROUND THE WORLD WHILE THE TRUTH IS STILL PUTTING ON ITS SHOES". You will start to notice changes in his energy and vibrations because of his frustrations. It's important that you try to preserve your heart while in the incipient stages with these guys. If you use the word "love", that's the code word to the womanizer to go in for the kill. Meaning sex, money, wash his clothes, pay his bills and so on. Until one day, he starts an argument over something that does not make sense to justify his exit. He knows that it's a matter of time before his armor comes off his body and face. He may often not be available which they use to try and manipulate your feelings to capitulation. If he does not get what he wants like a tick on a dog's back, he will fall off and look for other prey. If a real man is serious about you, he will wait until you are ready. The reason for the difference is because the real man is not afraid of falling in love. He realizes that anything in life worth having is often preceded by some degree of challenge. The womanizer views love as an adversary because he navigates in life in complete fear. She asked,

RECIPROCITY

"why are they this way?" I said, "there is no general answer". Showing love is a learned behavior, while making love is an innate behavior. Some come from families that failed to reinforce love, some saw their parents argue relentlessly as a child, some are children from divorced families and had no reinforcement. Some are just born psychopaths. The last thing is to understand that they both want love and love-making from you. The difference between the two is that, the normal guy is willing to give love back and the womanizer isn't. The last thing I wanted to talk to you about and I promise this is it. This is the life of the Coddler. Coddler men often grow up in unbalanced households with some mothers who felt compelled to overly nurture and coddled their sons to the point that they never developed independence. Many had fathers who were absent in their lives. When he tried to ride a bike, she said, "you may get hurt", when he tried to join the baseball team, she said, "you may get hit with the ball". She cleaned his dishes, wash his clothes, made his lunch, drove him to school until he was 17. This young man knows how to love. His problem is you could be turned off by the fact that his masculine energy has been contained in this web of emotions that he can't escape. In fact, his happiness relies on you so much that the minute you leave his sight he goes into a panic that's caused by feelings of insecurity. This type of man can be more dangerous than the womanizer because he depends upon you for his happiness which was conditioned by his coddled lifestyle. Most likely, he lacks confidence to the point that you have become his proxy mother. This man is nice and affectionate but unfortunately is still drinking his mother's breast milk. Everything in life requires a balance.

Top 5 Needs of Man and Woman

I believe that man and woman have 5 basic categories of essential and primary needs. Before I go further, I would like to differentiate between needs and wants. **"Needs"** are essential things needed for growth and function. **"Wants"** are more associated with the desire for non-essential things in life. I have listed these categories levels 1-5. For this chapter, please mentally remove your current lifestyle for the sake of this discussion and imagine yourself living as an aborigine in the outback of Australia. The reason I have to go here is that a man and woman's primary needs aren't segregated based on geography. I realize that the tangible items could be different but the overall needs are the same. I traveled to the Dominican Republic years ago for my sister's wedding. The day we arrived, 12 people in the wedding party decided to take a tour on rented ATVs on the back roads to experience the "DR" outside of the popular tourist spots. As we drove down these dirt streets, I noticed that many of the homes did not have roofs, some homes had partial roofs. Clothes were being dried on laundry lines in front and rear of the homes. Children ran out on the street as if we were international celebrities. As they approached, we emptied our pockets and handed money. We thought based on the way they lived that they needed it. Their smiles were bright, their personalities were jovial and their dispositions were gregarious, to say the least. You would have thought they won the power ball. How arrogant I must have been to assume that the warm welcome these children gave us was subject to us giving money. Obviously, I did not do a great job by emptying my mental cache of American-generated references. I told my mom at breakfast that it shows that our creator did not create happiness to be contingent upon what we accumulate in life. In 1959, after visiting India, Martin Luther King became extremely influenced and impressed by Mahatma Gandhi's writings, which became the message behind his non-violent approach for the sake of social change. Coretta Scott King talked about the fact that King did not believe in materialism so much that he refused to buy a home until she convinced him that it was necessary for the kids. The king family went 13 years before buying a home. King believed the way that Gandhi lived off the principles of asceticism. He was so committed to these principles that to his death, he had no public ownership of anything. Happiness is truly a choice not a lifetime discovery. Why would our creator make happiness subject to you having a million dollars or having a fancy car? Could our American wealth also be a hidden curse? Why do people who live in other parts of the world, areas that we would categorize as destitute seem to be much happier? While we thought they needed us because they were showing us how life is supposed to be. Give love and happiness to all you come in contact with, and through reciprocity, the world returns the same to you. Could reciprocity be the epicenter of serendipity? Oh, one other thing, their divorce rate is a lot better than ours. When I talk about the 5 needs of a man and woman, remember this represents humanity as a whole and not a particular lifestyle. A man who lives on the outskirts of the African Serengeti who wants to get his wife a Valentine's gift is not going to the hall mark store and get a card. Maybe, he created a pendant made out of clay with stones on the end that demonstrated his appreciation for her existence.

Men and Women are pre-wired and programmed to seek what I call, "level 1", these are **Water, Food, Shelter, Clothing**, in that order. Water is number 1 because we will die through osmosis and experience an organ break down, in about 5 days or less, if we are not properly hydrated. We die from the lack of nutrition in about 30 to

RECIPROCITY

45 days, depending on our body mass index (BMI). So, if you remember when I spoke in the chapter evolution of the 21st century woman, I spoke about women before the 1940s and before it gravitated to men who could demonstrate their certainty by being providers, loving, attentive, and a good wage earner. It did not hurt if he had a good benefit package as well. I created the "Cunningham Scale" or "C" scale. This is a scale I created for the sake of quantifying and prioritizing relationship value between men and women, that goes from the scale of 0 to 100. Most men before the 1940s got 70 points over 100, for their ability to satisfy the level 1 needs. This is the reason level 2 and beyond were neglected. They did not carry as much weight. Some men abused the fact that they were the only significant wage earner. They operated off of what I call the golden rule. "He who had the gold got to rule". I know of several baby boomer women who were fully aware of the consistent infidelity of their life partners but refused to act because they have been beaten down mentally for so long that any alternative was perceived as worst. Most men I believe were good honest family men who treated the fact that they were the primary wage earner as a privilege and treated their wives with dignity and respect. A good friend of mine was born in India. We were talking about how different our lives were as children. I spoke of building go-karts and bicycles from scratch. As we entered our teenage years, we repaired our cars. I never saw a repair shop until I was about 20. As teenagers with no financial responsibility, we had so much time that we would take a carburetor off our car and clean it with no hesitation. We would take appliance boxes and slide them down the hill. He said that most of his time was spent on the farm. They did not have a lot of mechanical machinery when cultivating the fields for the crops. I asked, "what did you use?" He replied, "we often used elephants to help us till the soil". I asked further, "how did you guys get them to stand still ?" From this point, the story got really interesting. He said, "when the elephants are first born, we tied a 6-foot rope around on one of the elephant's rear legs. They took the

other end and tied it to a 3-foot metal stake and hammered it in the ground. Whenever the elephants are not being walked, they would spend the first 3 years of life tied to this stake in the ground. He told me that after the third year and almost full size. The only thing they had to do to prevent the elephants from walking away was tie the rope around the leg. The elephant still believed that he could not move because he has been conditioned by the long-term effect of the rope on his leg. Information is not just power, it's everything. How many people do you know who continues to live in loveless households filled with dejection and pain on a daily basis, but refuses to leave because they believe that the rope is still tied to their leg? If you ever want to see what a person or government fears the most, you have to look no further than to see what or who is oppressed the most. For instance, women in Saudi Arabia are one of our greatest allies operating under a guardianship system. It was not until 2017 that women were just allowed to drive. Every woman in Saudi Arabia must have a guardian in her life. I make this point to shed light on the fact that this misogyny represented the majority of the world at some point in time. If society was not afraid of the power of women, why were they oppressed so much? The true answer is that they hold all the cards. The level one needs of men are the same as those of women That is, **"water, food, shelter, and clothing."** After level 1, we hit a fork in the road and things get very interesting. The feminine energy needs, on level 2, what I refer to as **Love, Affection, Attention, and Praise (LAAP).** The Level 2 needs for feminine energy are as important to feminine energy as gas is to your car. A good friend of mine ask me today, "why do you get your wife flowers every Friday?" I responded and said that, "I did not want a particular holiday or birthday to dictate when I address my appreciation for my life partner". Besides, she has a vase in her office and the flowers only last one week. He then asked, "what happens when she pisses you off?" I replied, "My friend, what I do for my wife is not contingent upon what she does for me. The reality of human nature is the fact that I can only manage what I do for her, it is not my responsibility to manage what she does for me. I express my demands through communication but it's up to her respond. Let's just call it relationship maintenance. I have found over the years that life flows so much easier when the positive energy that you deposit in life exceeds the energies that you receive". To me, this particular segment is probably the most difficult of them all. Many men believe that when their woman comes home from work stressed and asks, "can you lay down with me, cuddle under the sheets and watch a movie?", that becomes a code word for eventual penetration. This could be the case, but this is where communication is paramount. If you are in tune with her love language and energy you would be able to differentiate what her true needs were at that particular time. What she truly wanted was someone to offer her comfort and certainty. Look deep into her eyes and tell her no matter what happens in life, when you fall, I will always place myself in a position to comfort you and eliminate all your pain. Over the years, I have grown to realize how important "level 2" is to a woman. 10 years ago, I helped my wife build her corporate structure for her first business. When we filed her articles of incorporation, trade name, and operating agreements she began to display emotions. She said, "why isn't your name on it?" I replied, "I want you to have and feel complete control. I don't need to place my name on your articles to feel secure". This is not a leverage tool for eventual control. Giving hearts rarely concern themselves with the old saying, "what's in it for me?", when promoting you. Besides, I have enough business activities to keep up with. Overall, I feel compelled to grow with you in parallel, not in front and not behind, but in complete harmony. One of the things that I learned over the years is that money alone does not make us happy but growth does. If you are a man please remember that nothing turns a woman on more than a man who is constantly growing in every aspect of his life. I told someone recently that everything in life that stands still for long a period of time either corrodes or develops bacteria. It also applies to our relationships. In life, we are either growing or declining, there is no in-between. If you are not learning something new every day, you are losing, not gaining new life. In 2008 or so, I remember going to a John Maxwell business lecture in Orlando, Florida. I remember him saying that "poor leaders hoard power while great leaders give power away". He went on to say that, "insecure leaders are only concerned about empowering themselves but great leaders empower others". Over the years, I use a lot of my business teaching to augment myself and augment others. I try it to apply to my relationships as well. A true legacy is not based on what you do for yourself but the things you do for others. The statement that I'm about to make is directed to my male readers. I will highlight to make it more conspicuous because I don't want you guys to feel as if you have been left out. If you want to have a purposeful relationship filled with perpetual love, lust, and infatuation it is imperative that you focus a significant amount of your energy on level 2. Your failure to address level 2 consistently could jeopardize the overall health of your relationship in the long run. The level of thinking that has got you to where you are is insufficient to get you to where you are trying to go. As men, we often get misguided and believe that the way we see the world is congruent to hers. You could not be more incorrect. Don't get me wrong, most women love a nice day at the mall administering a dose of retail therapy. The house, car, dates, gifts, and trips are all secondary to level 2 needs. Oftentimes, we allow complacency to set in our relationships until it gets to the point that it becomes untreatable. A marital contract is not designed to tell you to administer perpetual love, affection, attention, and praise. Your job is to promote and honor your wife like a queen on a throne. The feminine energy is a hurricane of emotions. With all that I have studied, I can't tell you why my wife exhibits low energy some days and other days it's high. What I can tell you is that I stopped trying to figure it out. If you were able to figure it out you would be bored silly because predictable behavior lowers dopamine levels. It's not meant to be understood for several reasons. If you understood it, it would no longer be exciting. This may sound silly but the dates that I have with my wife that cost the least gives us the most. One of our exercise routes is walking across a very long bridge that joins Maryland and Virginia. The entire trip, including the trail, is about 5 miles. Our phones are turned off and the entire walk is only us and nature. You would be surprised how a simple walk could increase your listening and communication skills. These moments are necessary as we realign our vibrations, wavelengths, and energies. I call this "relationship recalibration" and must be done on weekly. We talked so much while walking you would have thought we just met. Life can be quite simple when you have two people who share the same goals economically, politically, environmentally, and spiritually. Let me give you an example. You meet someone interesting, your hormones and neurotransmitters are on overdrive. You are excited to the point of exhaustion. You fall in love, get married and 7 years into the relationship, it becomes lost because you never recalibrated new energies. Calibration is a lot like getting your wheels on your car balanced when you got the tires changed. When you don't balance your tires, you start to get vibration at higher speeds. Relationships operate very similarly. Same car different wheels. A good friend of mine received his law degree at 25 years old. By the time he was 30, he decided that he would stop practicing law because music was his passion. So, he started a Jazz Band and they are booked solid every night. He and his wife realigned energies so that his decisions weren't perceived as selfish. They are still married today because of their consistent support of each other. If you are a man and your wife met you early in life and the only thing you do is come home from work and play video games. Don't be surprised several years later if energies are thrown off course. Remember that the earth rotates about 1000 miles an hour. We live in an ocean of motion. Our bodies are molecular reservoirs that are always moving and evolving. What she accommodated and facilitated at 25 years of age may not be tolerable at 35 years of age. Men often marry women hoping that they will never change. Women often marry men hoping that they will. My life got easier when I stopped focusing on myself and started focusing on how I can extend my life beyond my death. The only way to achieve this is through your legacy. Here, I will tell you another story that is relevant to the importance of level 2 to a woman. Mariah Carey married a very wealthy record company executive, Tommy Mottolla, at the age of 24. Oftentimes, men think that giving lots of money and wealth is what most women want in life. She had anything she wanted except Level 2, (Love, affection, attention, and praise). Her first song after their divorce was a song titled "butterfly", which released on December 1, 1997. The song was written as a show of emotion and liberation from being coddled and mentally incarcerated. Her freedom was so important that the money meant nothing. Anytime the guys and I got together to play football; I was always the quarterback. When playing the quarterback position, it's important to throw the ball to a running receiver. You must throw to where the receiver is going and not where he is. If you throw to where he is, before the ball arrives, he will no be longer there. Relationships are often problematic because we tend to assess our mates based on where they are in life rather than where they are going. 7 years later, when you communicate, it feels like one speaks Mandarin and the other speaks Spanish. Love language adjustments should be made weekly. An example of this would be that you met your wife at a bar 6 years ago. Since then, she has obtained her law degree in international affairs. However, you still go to the same bar once a week and work at the same job. You refuse to learn, create, and invent anything new in life. Your failure to implement the laws of "Kaizen" in your life will inevitably cause a communication deficiency in your relationship. A reporter asked once Coretta Scott King what her reactions were when reports of her husband's infidelity surfaced. She said, "I married him for his vision in life and commitment for change". She married him based on where he was going not where he was. Please, when assessing your mate, make sure you take the time to understand the difference between vision and sight. Oftentimes, we use these two words synonymously but they have different meanings. Sight is the capacity to see the world on how it is, but Vision is the capacity to see the world on how it could be. Have you thrown the ball to a stationary object? Did you throw the ball to someone who views life as a bore and refuses to adopt an "I can do anything mentality"? Did you throw the ball to someone who refuses to permit themselves to fail and lives life in complete fear? Years ago, a little after the market crash of 2008. I asked my fiancée, who later became my wife, if she had something in mind that she wanted to do on her birthday. At that time, the global financial market was harder than a two-dollar steak. We were recovering financially because the bottom fell out the real estate market and loans were at a standstill. This was one of those years when I had a brain freeze and could not think of anything. I thought she would say a $3000 bag, a pair of red bottom shoes, a new car, pay off her student loans, a Caribbean get away and so on. Well, she threw me a curveball and I was expecting a fastball down the middle. She said, "you remember the park we used to walk near the stream in Washington, D.C?" "where we would watch the birds and squirrels?" I said, "yes, why do you ask?" She replied, "that is what I want to do". This taught me something very valuable that still holds today. Feminine energy that operates with integrity never places unnecessary financial pressure on their family for personal benefits. I'm always thinking of ways to augment my wife to expand her mentally and she teaches me how to do so as well. Also, I want to mention that it's important not to overindulge on feminine energy level 2. Overindulgence could lead to predictable behaviors, which could cause a loss in overall effectiveness. When a man addresses level 2 (LAAP), He not confuse being fully indulged in love, affection, attention, and praise so much that you forget to remain steadfast to who you are. Nothing is more unattractive to feminine energy than a man who lacks a backbone and certainty. There are people who tell you what you want to hear and people who will tell you what you need to hear. Offering support to my wife does not mean to acquiesce and capitulate to everything she asks. There has to be a balance. As I was writing this segment of my book, Apple sent a message that they are about to update my phone to stay ahead of the viruses and ensure optimum functionality. Well, that brings me to my next point. Why are you not downloading new software on your mental hard drive to reduce viruses and thoughts of infidelity? Why are many of us still operating on the 18, 19, and 20th century software and expecting your relationships to function with optimum efficiency? As times change, so does our relationship software. Men did not come home from work in 1920 and play Fortnite and Madden for 5 hours because they did not exist. Many men today are experiencing a social crisis because they are oblivious on how to consistently demonstrate respectful masculinity that a professional woman can appreciate and respect. As guys, you can never get caught up in how reciprocity works, you just have to embrace the process. With reciprocity, you have to always take the position as a victor and not a victim. When I take my wife to a play or a musical, it's the play and the musical that gets the attention. When we walk into our favorite park near the stream, the attention is on us. The 21st century man has hard choices to make. Your skill sets have to be modified for today's professional women. There is an old saying that goes, "I can do bad by myself". Well, the 21st century woman says "I can do good by myself". My friend, you can no longer address level one needs because she has it covered. The things that cost the least will often give you the most. We get complacent and forget the little things that interest us in the first place. We must never forget the little things. Hormones and neurotransmitters are God's work, but you got credit for it. In the second year and beyond, the requirement for relationship skills is needed. Married men often complain about not getting enough sex and married women often complain about not getting enough love. These areas of concern are often overlooked because most people are oblivious to relevant relationship tools. These are ever-evolving love languages. If you are not listening and operating on the same vibration and wavelength, you can easily miss your station and the music gets distorted. When my last son was born, I got the opportunity to hold him for the first time in the hospital. The nurse helped me with the pamper while my wife was asleep. I took the blanket and wrapped my son and it looked great to me. She said, "no that's incorrect sir", with her raspy voice. I'm thinking, "how difficult can that be, besides I've run over 10 companies". The nurse grabbed the blanket and pulled apart all my work and began to restructure it. She started to fold the blanket symmetrically in so many areas that I had to study it on YouTube before I got it right. When she finished, the blanket was tucked like the baby was in a cocoon. For me, this process is probably on the same parallel as folding fitted sheets. That was when I learned that there are differences between cuddle and coddle. A baby fresh out of the mother's womb needs to feel coddled, to simulate the comfort and security that an amniotic sac gives an infant. Cuddle is defined as, **"holding in one's arms as a way to show love and affection"**. This is an element of Level 2. We must not get it confused with the element of coddled, which is defined as **"treating in an indulgent or overprotective way"**. This is the man that says that I don't want you to lift a finger. He does everything to the point of obsession. I felt compelled to use this experience so that my men readers don't feel the need to overindulge in the process. Trying to coddle someone long-term could have an adverse reaction. I have to make this distinction because overindulgence is one of the most insidious forms of abuse.

The Level 3 needs of a Woman

The Level 3 needs of a woman are what I call "DGT", which stands for dates, gifts, and trips. Most men inadvertently place level 3 needs in level 2 position. They assume since most women enjoy shopping, more dates, gifts, and trips could only intensify happiness and enjoyment. This is the guy who would typically tell his friends that "I give her everything and she still complains." What he does not realize is the fact that women are appreciative of the date, gifts, and trips. However, Love, Affection, Attention, and Praise, which are positioned at level 2 needs, cannot be supplemented with currency. It has to be administered with your presence. I have a very financially successful couple that I have known for some time. One day, the husband said to me, "Ed, I don't know what is wrong, I literally give my wife anything she wants. She never has to ask twice. I purchased a very large home, diamond bracelets, a new car, trips to Dubai, renovated the entire kitchen in just the last year, and she does not seem to appreciate anything". I asked, "what version do you want. The church version or the bar version?" He said, "give it to me straight". I replied "Tony she does appreciate all that you do, but you are never f _ _kin home". I said, "look here, love is intangible, it's not something that you can buy. You can't put a price tag on time spent. It is called relationship equity. I tell you with all certainty if you get off your ass pick your wife up in the car and drive her to the park, sit down on a bench, and watch the ducks wade in the water. It will have a greater effect than the bracelet you bought for her last week". I said, "love should not be just a word, it should be a subject matter.

It's much more complicated than the sorry definition given to us by the dictionary. Love is about behavior, responsibility, accountability, respect, integrity, and presence. When you stop confusing what you want with what she wants, you will get better results. Stop trying to buy your wife's love and get off your ass and partake in her life. When you make those changes, life will change for you". I told someone the other day that kids remember more of what you do with them than for them. Spend more time with her and less time chasing money. Next, I want you to take her shopping and a candlelight dinner. Leave your phone in the trunk of the car. I want 100% of your attention to be on your wife throughout the night and communicate with her like it is a new date. I don't want this to be a temporary event but rather your new identity. You have a choice, continue to live life the way you are and possibly cause future resentment and demise. I want this to be your new domestic identity. In the past, you would just give her the money and send her on her way. This time I want you to be immersed in the process. The same thing you did to get her is necessary to keep her. I said, "look Tony, you have done well for yourself. You have great earnings, credit, and demonstrated great leadership and financial comfort for your family. I just need you to segregate financial support from the primary needs of a woman". I was not always in this mental space. Over the years, I've learned through the study of psychology and sociology. I really don't like shopping as well. I still don't know the difference between a dam stiletto and a pump. However, when my wife came out of the dressing room of a clothing store the other day and asked me, "Honey, how do I look?" I said, "fantastic honey, I'm going to tear you up when we get home", as she laughed her way back in the dressing room. Financial success means nothing if your presence is contained in a dark cavern.

Levels 2 and 3 needs of a Man

Before I go further, let me conduct a quick recap. The Level 1 Primary needs of a Man are Water, Food, Shelter, and Clothing (WFSC), Level 2 is Challenge, while Level 3 is Acknowledgement. Challenge and acknowledgment have a synergistic relationship. A study was conducted by a sociologist years ago at an elementary school. They separated a group of 5-year-old boys and girls during recess. In one of the classrooms, they placed all the boys and in the other classroom they placed all the girls. Audible recordings were conducted of the classrooms for 45 minutes. After the recordings, they attempted to differentiate words from sounds. This study revealed that in the classroom that contained girls, (81%) of what they heard were words, and (19%) were sounds. The class room that contained boys (78%) of what they heard were sounds and (22%) were words. If you get the opportunity to take your young children to a playground, watch carefully the activity of boys and girls. Young boys typically engage in activity that offers challenge and the ability to compete. Like Racing, who jumps the highest from the bars, who climbs the highest on the vertical rope. who has the best backward flips, etc.? The interesting thing is that these activities occur way before social conditioning begins to influence the child. Young girls play on the same playground equipment, but they don't typically engage with the playground equipment with the same competitive enthusiasm as the boys. The girls use the equipment for enjoyment and prove to themselves that they can accomplish different activities. This has absolutely nothing to do with capabilities. We all know that the girls are capable of executing the same task as the boys. Boys turn the playground into child Olympics. Boys take any opportunity to create separation from mediocrity. Any of my readers who have 2 boys around the same age can tell you that they often sound like they are going to tear a hole in the wall. My wife asked me today, while I was out running with my son, "when you guys are engaging in activities, why does he get upset whenever you finish first in activities such as brushing teeth, walking up the steps, running in the park, and so on?" She said, "I don't want him to feel that he has to win everything in life to be successful". I said that he will evolve and learn how to differentiate between winning and losing later in life. Today he is only 4 years old, and he is wired by our creator to seek challenges and win. When growing up, my dad absolutely refused to use directions to put things together. It was like an insult for a man to use directions to put together simple household items such as furniture, toys, equipment, and so on. My wife and her friend went out to eat crabs at a local hot spot. She said that several men offered to buy their meals and drinks. Jokingly, I said, did they do the same for others in their proximity. She said, "no" and I said, "why you?" She responded, "he was being nice, I guess". I said, "he could have been nice before you got there". The point I'm trying to make is men need good deeds to receive acknowledgments. Good deeds are stored like casino chips and traded in for an opportunity to gain social pleasures. By no means does this mean that every man's actions are induced solely for sexual satisfaction. A man does not want acknowledgment, he needs it. You can't receive acknowledgment unless you successfully conquer your challenge. Social pleasures come in different categories such as dates, intimacy, and sex. I believe that a man is placed here to please a woman with anything she allows him to. When I created the 5 top needs of men and women, my goal was to identify why masculine energy typically responds to challenges and feminine energy responds to praise and attention. As I studied masculine energy, I realized that so much of nature responds the same way. Male Lions fight for male dominance

LEVELS 2 AND 3 NEEDS OF A MAN

in a bid to lead the pride, male Hippos fight over territory in and along the Nile river, male Deer grows full antlers specifically for brawling with each other during their mating seasons. After the mating season ends, the antlers fall off and the process starts over again. It is made complete because we have the same creator. Masculine energy requires challenges on a daily basis. It is not a want, it is a need. One of the ever-evolving daunting tasks that 21st century professional women is faced with today is learning how to assess the talent and skill set of today's men. The current social paradigm shift is causing necessary adjustments to be made to maintain domestic polarity. Women I have spoken to want to relinquish necessary power, to appease the interest of their partners. But in most cases, they express concern that weak men have no vision or direction, which makes it difficult. Remember in the 19th and much of the 20th century, there was never a challenge because the woman's financial role was more limited domestically. I have a friend whose wife earns about 110 thousand dollars a year and he earns about the same salary. He vents to me that anything he wants to do around the house, his wife always has to get involved and tell him how she thinks it's supposed to be done. When a woman impedes or refuses to relinquish complete autonomy to a man, the opportunity to work around the house and complete other tasks could jeopardize polarity levels to the point a man could develop inadequate feelings. When this happens, symptoms that may arise are typically low energy, depression, extra jobs, staying late at the office, and so on. He subconsciously participates in as much external activity as possible so he does not have to be in the presence of his wife. His wife has become so overbearing that her presence feels less of a wife and more of a mother. Early in our relationship, my wife struggled with somethings that I would do around the home until I told her one day that, "I need you to remove your past from the present". I am not going to jeopardize our family guessing whether something is done right. I told her that I was raised around very strong masculine men that exposed me to a lot. She apologized and said that she was not used to the level of certainty that I display daily. In the past, she had to take on a lot of those responsibilities because of inadequate trust levels. Some women don't relinquish complete autonomy because they don't have total trust in their partners' abilities or decision-making. My wife today does not worry about when I say I'm going to clean the pool, cut the grass, paint a room, check the air pressure on the tires, change a bad electrical receptacle, etc. I told my wife a decade ago that I know you are used to seeing me in a suit, but getting dirty does not frighten me. Besides, I've flipped some of my own investment properties. Ladies, I know that you are fully capable and aware of how to change tires, take out the trash, cut the grass, and so on, but It's important, especially in today's relationship climate, that you understand that a man is wired to engage in challenging activity. It's a part of his innate point system. When you interrupt his ability to accumulate points, it throws off his energy. Nothing depresses a masculine man more than the inability to provide for his family. Men feed off acknowledgment as plants feed off sunshine. Men wake up looking for a smiling woman because he is programmed to take the path of least resistance. If she is smiling then there is less work to be done in his quest for social pleasures. One summer morning, my wife went to the store in a form-fitting sweatsuit to get a few items before breakfast. She told me of how several store employees and non-employees offered her help in the aisles. So, the question becomes, why were these men so helpful? Why do men always ask women if they need help almost compulsively? Could they be acting out the way they were raised to be overall gentlemen? Yes, this could be the case, but not with most. When growing up, I never saw a male figure in my life that asked for directions to anywhere. Getting your wife or friend to the destination without directions on your own was an opportunity to be rewarded with level 3, acknowledgment. If somehow, all women moved to the moon, men would probably quit their jobs the next day. There would be no one to acknowledge their accomplishments. Many times, I hear or see really successful women who can't seem to keep anyone around for any significant. In many cases, their personalities and energy exude so much masculine energy and control that they can't find a suitable partner that's willing to facilitate this type of polar imbalance. Many men began to feel mentally incarcerated. Without challenge, there could be no acknowledgment, and without acknowledgment there can't be exchange for social and intimate pleasures. Statistically, a man thinks about sex over 19 times a day. I was watching my business channel last year and heard that a few of the popular porn channels received a 50% increase in traffic during a major snowstorm. When men get bored, sex, sports, and video games are top options. One thing that we can never argue is that our God spent a lot of time creating ways to ensure that the human race propagated and proliferated perpetually. What does a woman possess that creates such innate reactions from men all over the earth? I promise not to exaggerate on this point. Overall, men want to feel appreciated and acknowledged. When your man loses his job and his ability to take care of his family is jeopardized, what he needs most is your uninterrupted support. Let him know how difficult life would be if he was not there. I don't mean from a monetary perspective but a life perspective. Most men that I have spoken to, who have indulged in extra-marital affairs, often complain about the lack of quality intimacy and sex. Men don't want to feel like a stranger in their bedroom. As women try to address this demand, a mental block on how he neglects her level 2 continues to be the driving force behind her reluctance to just let go. The arguments and contentious discussions can't have impact on intimacy. I don't curse a lot, so my wife thinks it's funny when I do. I will tell this particular story uncensored for the sake of authenticity. Before we got married, my wife and I went on a business appointment with some long-time clients that I've known for years. I was speaking to the husband and my wife spoke to his wife in another room. My wife knew that they have been married for years and wanted to get some advice from a successfully married couple. If I had known, I would have told my fiancée at the time that his wife speaks whatever comes to her mind. My wife asked her because she is older and more seasoned. My wife asked her, "what are your secrets to keeping a happy husband, home, and successful marriage?" She told my wife, "You know girl, I fuck my husband until he can't walk every chance I get". She said, "many women use sex as a leverage tool and wonder why their man never comes home on time". "If you don't, somebody else will". It works for me because I always get what I want. My wife was embarrassed by the response because she was expecting something cleaner. There is a lot of truth to her answer, however, when I created the top 5 needs of a woman and a man. The second need of any man is intimacy and sex. The reason that it's not level 2 is that his capture rate is significantly reduced because most respectful women require a respectable process. This is why men have to seek the challenge. It was initially difficult for me to live by these principles until I decided to realize that my focus should be on how to improve myself. I know use the word "reciprocity" a lot, but I have to be consistent on the point of how important one must be when depositing positive energy to someone who is not fulfilling your overall needs. I equate this commitment to getting saved in a church. You absolutely can't get involved in what someone is not doing for you, because it's not your responsibility. I hear countless couples talk about I'm giving 100% and he is only giving 50%. Who in the hell made you the relationship statistician? It's never going to end because you are keeping your score from your perspective. It does not work like that. What works is to be the best wife you can be, irrespective of what your partner does. They will either respond or your frequency and vibrations will be realigned. Ladies, if you want to be of assistance in offering confidence to your husband, especially, if your income contributions are congruent to each other. You have to make sure that you are conscientious to levels 2 and 3 needs of a man. The failure of your husband or partner to feel relevant in your union could cause energies to be contaminated by external forces. This is important because most men don't have a clue. Typically, they don't pick up books on relationships, and as a result, they will likely be led by internal frequencies aligning them to someone else that gives them maximum polarity.

The Levels 4 and 5 needs of men and women

Levels 4 and 5 needs of men and women are the same, but how we arrived at the same conclusion is quite different. Man and woman share the same elements of level 4, which is intimacy. When you are committed to long-term relationships, it's important to realize that predictability is not your friend. Starting today, I want you to no longer view your bedroom as just a place to sleep and have sex. I want you to see your bedroom more like it's "50 shades of grey". I have LED lights behind my headboard. In fact, I'm getting ready to install a small smoke machine under my bed. I know you may be excited by my ideas but remember this. Relationships don't end because of the lack of love; they end due to the lack of intimacy. If the fire and juice has dissipated out of your relationship, nobody else is to be blamed, except fault the people who are involved. My wife knows that any piece of furniture is always a possibility. I refuse to ever be so predictable that my wife knows everything I will do. I realize that there are days or nights when the desire to satisfy immediate needs is greater than the time necessary to create theatrics and productions. The point that I'm trying to make is the fact that we are wired to seek novelty. When sex becomes predictable, dopamine levels start to plummet. There are so many sex games and toys that can extend your enjoyment and maintain novelty that you can buy online. I'm always looking for new things to surprise my wife with. Sex, especially when you spend time on a trip on vacation or staycation, should be more of a production than an act. My wife does not know this, but the next time we go out of town, I'm going to jump out of the closet in a

RECIPROCITY

firefighter coat and a helmet and put her fire out. This is how serious intimacy should be for you. Your failure to add excitement could lead to complacency. You thought you could go for 15 years with a little oral sex, you on top, she on top, a little from the back, and go to sleep was going to lead you to a life of perpetual sexual satisfaction. The worst thing you can do is lie to yourself. Some male associates and I were talking about relationships one day. One of the guys spoke about how difficult it was to get his wife to have sex with him. He said I'm responsible, I take care of my responsibilities, I feel I'm a great father and husband. So, the question he asked was, "if I'm the same person, same penis, same height, and maybe 20 pounds heavier why does she respond emotionless". I told him that, "I really don't have an answer for you because I don't have enough information". I said what I can tell you is the fact that this evolved and you never recognized the signs. A marital contract will never supersede our bodies, both chemically and emotionally. If you want quality intimacy, my friend, you are going to have to work at it every day. Go back to the days when you first met and mentally start dating all over again. Any normal human seeks love by default, what shapes our behavior is love and where we get it from. If you want that erotic sexual excitement you had when you first started to date, you are going to have to create it before someone else does. Many adulterous affairs have nothing to do with the fact that they have good responsible spouses in place. You can be the nicest person in the world and still starve for passion and intimacy. Are you just going through the motions because it's your marital responsibility? You must expand your sexual knowledge and understand what your partner's needs are. My wife knows that when I'm with her. I'm always serious. She narrates the story of how we went to Colorado and stayed in the Gaylord, Colorado Springs, at the foot of the golf course and a backdrop of some beautiful Colorado mountains. I can only tell you that we started our intimate moments around midnight and went to bed an hour before the sun came up. We actually missed the first part of our convention. Every day was planned in detail from visiting one of the highest peaks in Colorado, Pikes Peak. Tours, and shows. This activity is what I call "incipient lovemaking". Sex for couples who have been together for a while does not have to be difficult. The difficulty surfaces when we forget how we got here in the first place. Never stop dating your partner. Intimacy and sex were put here for your enjoyment so don't take them for granted.

Physiology of Attraction

This particular chapter is one of my favorites, because I feel this is where a great deal of separation occurs from traditional relationship books. As I studied who I was on a cellular and chemical level, this allowed me to identify biological markers that have significant influence over our daily emotions and beyond. I learned in one of my college psychology classes titled "Theories of Personality" that our personalities are fully established before the age of 7 and 70% of our self-esteem is developed before the age of 9. When I made the earlier reference to Aristotle quote "Give me a child until he is 7 and I will show you the man" derived from what he knew about child development. Before I dive deeper, I am cautious on how in depth I choose to be in this chapter because I don't want to lose my readers with an abundance of physiological science facts. After all this is a relationship book. I would be remised however if I refrain from exposing you to the internal wiring that plays such a significant role in most of our relationship decisions. What I don't want you to do, is to learn these facts and principles to justify your behavior and say that's why I'm like this because dad was never here. This is not my intent or message. In fact, trying to justify your actions could exacerbate an already precarious situation. Some neurotransmitters and hormones have a significant influence on our decision-making daily. Let me first differentiate between a neurotransmitter and a hormone. Neurotransmitters are produced in the brain and hormones are produced by various organs and secreted in the bloodstream. When I first met my wife as she sat on the other side of a table.

She reminded me of seen in the movie "Basic Instinct" starring "Sharon Stone". Sexy, seductive, smart, and very charismatic. She denies this overwhelming sex appeal, but I know what I felt. I would say that our energies were congruent with each other. The reason I have to expound on this experience is that at this moment I know nothing about her. I believe that the foundation of what I call the "Automation phase" which is 90% lust, is based on the fact that we are wired to reproduce and propagate. Initial attraction or engagement is driven chemically and requires very little effort on your part. If we did not have this overwhelming emotion, I assure you that the world would have half the people we currently have. I once had a male agent that worked for me. He told me that he was going to attend an outdoor concert on a Saturday. I said have a great time hope you and your wife have a great time. He took a few steps forward and turned around and said it's not my wife and that he will ask God for forgiveness. The way that he said it was almost as if sex had controlled his life. He blamed his actions on the fact that his value and belief system had been seriously compromised. I don't know how long it took our creator to create the human species, but one thing is for sure when he thought about how he could ensure that we would all reproduce and propagate by associating the best feeling in the world with reproduction he hit the jackpot. Let's take a quick peek. First, he made it so that lust would influence you significantly when you noticed someone that you were attracted to. Once intimacy is established it is often followed by sex. Friction during sex stimulates various hormones and neurotransmitters that stimulate the process of orgasm. This was absolutely masterful. A male associate I know told me that his wife filed for divorce. I said if you don't mind me asking, what is the reason. He said his wife answered his phone and spoke to a woman who said that they have been intimate recently and he never disclosed that he was in an existing marriage. He said his wife asked him why did you do this, he said I don't know, it just happened. The "just happened" answer has become quite popular for centuries.

I told him that you, unfortunately, allowed 12 years of marriage and two children to be exposed to the temptation of external energies. He is being truthful; it did just happen. The reason it happens is that there were no stopgap systems in place. Hormones won the battle over his value and belief systems. I said there are people that I meet that may innately create a surge in attraction, but I don't act on the impulse because my value and belief systems are always reinforced on a daily basis. This allows me to walk away from these random lustful temptations that surface from time to time. A male friend of mine dated a married woman who would stop by his home every Friday just for sex. She told him that she is happy in her marriage and would be devasted if he found out. She always told her husband that she and the girls would stop by happy hour and have a couple of drinks. He told me that she would take some of his alcohol and put it in her mouth to simulate drinking to corroborate her story. Sex by far is the most powerful temptation known to man. Do the names Harvey Weinstein, Bill Cosby, R Kelley, Matt Lower ring a bell. If I took my time, I could come up with another 50 including school teachers, priests, pastors, etc. These are a few men, without question, who were at the pentacle of success in their professional industry. They all have or had endless money and probably did not have a problem with someone committing to be their life partner. The great Mark Twain once said that a "lie can travel halfway around the world while the truth is still putting on its shoes". How could such successful men place themselves in such precarious positions over love and intimacy? The answer is quite simple. When you present sexual desire in conjunction with psychopathic or sociopathic behavior, this is a recipe for a disaster. I'm going to touch on this quickly without getting off track. Let me quickly make this point and please write it down because it should be a part of your relationship checklist personal or business. Psychopaths are born that way and sociopaths evolve that way from their environment. A psychopath could also be a sociopath, but a sociopath is not necessarily a psychopath. This means that many guys who exhibit this type of behavior have no conscience. Therefore, most of their actions become almost serial. A normal man would have difficulty achieving an erection during a sexual assault because the excitement activates the sympathetic nervous system causing blood flow to poor to extremities, not sex organs. The abnormal man operates in a parasympathetic nervous system state because he has no feelings and lacks empathy. Having non-consensual sex is like sitting on a beach listening to a rising tide. Our conscious mind acts like a filtration system that allows us to differentiate right from wrong. I'm not making excuses for these guys, however, the behavior is without question abnormal, to say the least.

Have you ever seen one of these murder shows and hear a true psychopath describes where he placed the dead bodies and he sounds like he's walking in a park listening to his favorite music? This is classic psychopathic behavior apathy in its pure form. Also, I want to differentiate between Borderline Personality Disorder and Bi Polar Disorder. Bi-Polar disorders are mood disorders and (BPD) is a personality disorder, it is a short version. Many people get it confused, or almost use these terms synonymously. I am sympathetic to those who truly suffer from either one of these diseases. I am not suggesting that these personality and mood disorders can't be coped with. My purpose is to shed light on ways in which many of these conditions can be identified early in a relationship so that you are aware before you decide to commit your life. This is why I support living together for about 6 months before you decide to get married. This helps you to witness several cycles of psychological and physiological imbalances that can often be suppressed when dating. When you live together, it's more difficult to suppress mood imbalances consistently. Bi-polar disorders are characterized by extensive mood swings from a state of euphoria to depression in minutes. When operating in a state of euphoria they often indulge in spontaneous, risky, and impulsive behavior. Life is processed at a very high pace and the need for sleep is significantly reduced. In their depressive state, they often feel just the opposite. Tired, unenthusiastic, depressed, and feelings of hopelessness. This person will often depend upon their partners for their happiness which could be dangerous depending on the severity. Let me divulge into the condition called Borderline Personality Disorder or (BPD). People with (BPD) often experience difficulty in managing their emotions and are extremely sensitive to the smallest things they embark on in life. They often have thoughts of feeling abandonment which is why they are more likely to stay in abusive relationships because they are often self-critical of not being enough. Also, they become extremely dependent to their partners for complete happiness. I know of a gentleman who attended grade school with me. He had no drug or arrest history, and attended church every Sunday. One day, his wife decided that it was time for her to move on to something else in life and the next day she was found dead. It's important that you realize that you don't have a partner that depends solely on your presence for their happiness. It could put your life in a very precarious position. A Harvard University Love Study conducted by several doctors in the area of the biology of love categorized this process in 3 basic stages, which includes; Lust (the incendiary process), sex, and intimacy. Many people may not realize this, but early in the process of conception, if the (Y) chromosome from a man fertilizes a female egg which is (X), the new union becomes (XY). This triggers a complicated process causing the woman's embryotic gonads which, would have normally produced ovaries to produce testicles instead. If the (X) chromosome from a man fertilizes an egg of a woman this would cause the female gonads to remain the same and produce a female. The point that I'm making is the fact that a male's testes come from the exact same embryotic gonads during conception. This is what I believe is the epicenter of lust and pure sex with the secretion of estrogen and testosterone. A woman's ovaries produce estrogen and progesterone while a man's testicles produce testosterone. Women sometimes express the fact that they experience increase in vaginal secretions and an increased heart rate when in proximity of someone they are attracted to. When lust elevates and engages, it adds on another layer called "attraction", which causes the secretion of dopamine and serotonin. I want to spend a little time explaining these two neurotransmitters because, I think you will find their functionality extremely useful after reading this book. To start with, in explaining Dopamine, there are hundreds of websites on the internet that are specifically catered to marital affairs. Many people often ask why don't they just leave. The reason they won't leave is because the many affairs in relationships have nothing to do with the fact that they have a good, hard working, responsible, attractive, mentally stable spouse at home. Many affairs occur out of the need for dopamine. I know of a married gentleman who routinely meets with a married woman once a week. They both indicated that they are happily married. All bills are paid, children are happy, houses and cars are up to date. Overall, both relationships, at least from the surface, are functional. The reason they feel compelled to rendezvous once a week for social pleasures is what I believe is depleted dopamine and serotonin levels in their marriage. In other words, their marriage has lost its flame. In the long run, this behavior will lead to a path of destruction and possible resentment. The novelty and newness of an affair gives them a fix. like a drug that ultimately stimulates them chemically. The affair continues because they have no idea on how to restore the passion and purpose in their marriage and domestic lives. If they suddenly had to live together, they probably would not last for 30 days. The fact that they meet in local hotels and nonexistent business trips is an excitement in and of itself. Sex is actually the peak of the affair. After sex dopamine plummets, and the process starts all over again. Dopamine is responsible for anticipation, motivation, and desire. One weekend in January, I took my wife on an impromptu trip to the Pocono Mountains. I did not tell her where we were going, I just told her what attire she needed, and of course lingerie a man's best friend. We arrived in the middle of the night and the temperature was 2 degrees and snowy. After checking in, I opened the door to our 3-level suite. there was a glass floor that over looked a heated pool on the lower level. To the right was a wood burning fireplace. The second level featured a round shaped bed with mirrored head board and a heart shaped hot tub with power jets for maximum pleasure overlooking a beautiful mountain lake. Also, the lower level had a sauna in the same room as our pool. Champagne on ice was already placed in the room by guest services. I set my phone play list on "love jams". Later on, I took an entire bottle of body oil and rubbed my wife down until my hands became numb. As the music played, we entered the heated pool almost in slow motion like a music video. I grabbed my wife and kissed her on every level until my lips became swollen. I dove underwater and began…sorry I can't tell you more because I may be forced to put in the dog house, I'm sure you get the message. Love making that night with my wife was nothing short of fantastic. This happened about 10 years of being together. This is not a want, it's a requirement to maintain sustainable levels of dopamine. I felt compelled to share this personal story because it's necessary to convey how the simple things in life means so much. I work on my marriage everyday like a crossword puzzle because the alternative could lead to a loveless household filled with dejection and stress. Dejection and stress create opportunity to foreign invasion in the form infidelity and other irresponsible behavior. No one can guarantee how long a relationship will last, but one thing is for sure, it will certainly end much sooner if the simple things are not given adequate attention. Contrary to popular belief, your marriage and what you contribute must be assessed weekly. If I had asked my wife and said, "honey, your mom has our son this weekend would you like to go out of town somewhere. She would have enjoyed the idea but the dopamine levels would not have been impacted the same way as the way that it was packaged. A study was conducted years ago on dopamine levels in rats. Wires were attached to a couple of rats during this study. The two rats were initially fed food pellets and the dopamine levels elevated significantly. The next day they fed the rats again and the rats dopamine levels spiked again. Later in the experiment they decided to feed the rats the same time every day while they recorded dopamine levels. After feeding the rats the same day and the same time for a week they noticed that the dopamine levels started to plummet. This reveals a very interesting dynamic that predictability decreases anticipation and as a result, it lowers a very key ingredient that's responsible for everything in life that gives us excitement and the joy of anticipation. If we did not have dopamine, the desire to innovate, create, travel, date, work and so on would be non-existent. God knew one thing for sure, if he wants to get us off our ass, he needed a self-stimulating neurotransmitter that could biologically create an environment, if managed properly, would cause us to want more out of life. If we did not have dopamine, we would all sit around feeling depressed. For instance, addiction occurs when dopamine and serotonin levels are extremely high. Cocaine and alcohol addiction are directly associated with elevated dopamine and serotonin levels. Cocaine puts dopamine on steroids which is why it is so addictive. When the drug replaces the body's ability to self-generate dopamine on its own, the body depends upon the production of dopamine in the drug and not you. I personally get this from running. Some may call it "runners high". I love how running makes me feel when I'm done. If you have ever fallen in love with another person it could not be possible without the presence of dopamine. Do you really think billionaire Jeffrey Epstein had to rape women to get satisfaction? Of course not, these psychopath sex predators get a dopamine surge off the process of control until it becomes addictive. Ladies it is imperative, especially in relationships on the other side of 7 years, that you don't become complacent in your relationships. Men enjoy being turned out every now and then. It lets them know you are still there. Find arrangements for the kids and plan a weekend and don't tell him where he is going. When you get there, show him some moves that he's never seen before. He will love the fact that you took

PHYSIOLOGY OF ATTRACTION

the time to orchestrate such a fabulous weekend. This is for my men readers. I always say be respectful and always unpredictable. I get my wife flowers every Friday. I take her on a trip every three months, even if it's for a couple days. I focus on the things she has not done and places she has not been to. I'm always exploring new sex positions, new restaurants, new places to travel. If your wife or girlfriend knows everything that you are going to do for her before you do it, you are doing something wrong. It's January. and I just managed to hide a brand-new LandRover Velar from her in the garage for a few days before Christmas. I told her that the floors were painted and the fumes were really bad. How do you expect to excite your woman when you base what you do for her on the presence of a national holiday? Why does a national holiday have to dictate when you do something your wife can be excited about? Three years ago, I took my wife to Vegas, for just 3 days. On the first day, I arranged for a Limo to pick us up from the mirage hotel and drive us to the airport. There we boarded a red helicopter that flew over the Vegas strip, then we flew over the hoover dam and later flew down into the rim of the grand canyons, then we wrapped it up with a lunch. It was one of the best excursions I ever experienced. The next morning, we drove ATVs on the dessert. I'm giving you these examples because these are the things that are necessary to maintain excitement especially in long term relationships. Never assume that the marital vows are sufficient to maintain a healthy relationship. As men, I want to stress the importance of trying to maintain adequate testosterone as you grow in age. The average man loses about 2% testosterone per year for every year after the age of 25. Belly fat increases estrogen levels in men which accelerates testosterone decline. My point is that you have to work twice as hard when you are excising as you get older, even more than you did when you were younger, to achieve better results, Testosterone has always been man's best friend. Another important chemical that we all produce is serotonin. I refer to Serotonin as a hybrid chemical. It's not just a neurotransmitter but also a hormone.

Let me divulge, 92% of our serotonin is produced in the gut and 8% is produced in the brain. The gut and brain have a synergistic relationship. Serotonin is responsible for how we feel, our mood, and energy. One day, I had to talk to my wife about a very contentious subject that had the tendency of becoming very serious. Whenever I have moments like this, I always make sure that she is not hungry or at the wrong time of the month. My wife does not suffer from PMS, but I will say she may not have the best of moods. I have witnessed women who truly suffer from PMS. Let's just say that it's not a room you would want to be in for a long period of time. Most women who truly suffer from PMS actually experience a decrease of serotonin in most cases prior to that time of the month which causes them to be extremely irascible. When the cycle ends, the serotonin levels return to normal and the sun comes back out. When some women are hungry, low sugar levels causes disruption in hormonal balance, which causes irritability as well. When we are attracted to someone, serotonin tends to spike because their presence makes us feel good. Much like a drug that has addictive qualities. This is why some people can't handle breakups very well because the serotonin is influenced by the presence of the other person. Serotonin is the epicenter of our mood and feelings. Someone once said that, "if you want to assess the character of the person you are with, pay close attention to how they treat people they don't need because that's you next". If they treat everyone they meet and greet with integrity and compassion, chances are they will do the same with you. If they treat people apathetically and lacks compassion, it's a very good chance that you are next. People who truly suffer from bi-polar disorders typically have severe fluctuations in serotonin levels. This is why shacking up for 6 months has its benefits sometimes. Dating alone for 6 months may not give you the opportunity to witness and experience fluctuating patterns that you need to be aware of. We can't hide congenital disorders forever and at some point, who we are will inevitably reveal itself. Let me go on record and say that I truly don't have any bias towards those who may suffer from chemical imbalances because most can be managed with proper medications such as Prozac and Lithium. I just prefer to know what the circumstances are before committing to someone that does not fit in my long-term life plans. The other thing that I want to discuss is how your health, specifically your gut, has a direct impact on your daily mood and your overall motivation. Before you complain to your partner about what they are not doing, it's important to first focus on yourself. Just because you eat a tasty dinner and your belly is full does not mean that you are adequately nourished. The Adequacy levels of the neurotransmitter serotonin is the most important thing in our entire body system. It must remain at adequate levels so that your happiness does not become someone else's property. Our body does not necessarily crave food, our body only craves the nutrients that are found in food. After the body metabolizes our food by absorbing the necessary nutrients, the rest is purged out in our stool. Our digestion system is spread out over a long area and if opened, it could cover two tennis courts. If you have a leaky gut and the foods that you eat are not being processed efficiently, lesions can develop in the digestion track causing leakage in the blood stream. This can cause cell inflammation, inflammatory bowel disease, and auto immune diseases. Let me tell you a quick story. I have always been athletic and worked out consistently. As I mentioned early in the book. I run and work out consistently. I started to take a teaspoon a day of apple cider vinegar, 6-8 glasses of water daily, probiotics of at least 30 billion cultures. My smoothie consists of wheat grass, sea moss, slices of apples, lemon, berries, bananas and spring water, ginger and cinnamon. My weight, about the time I started, was about 190 lbs., and my height was 5'10". 2 weeks after, I noticed that my energy level had elevated and I would forget to eat because my body was nutritionally fulfilled. The interesting thing is the fact that my weight stayed the same primarily because I still continued to eat healthy meals and lifted weights. Later, I had to donate 8 of my business suits because they no longer fit. My abs became more defined and ripped almost like my school days. The reason I have to spend time here is because your entire mood and attitude towards life is directly influenced on the back of a healthy microbiome. If 92% of the hormone serotonin is produced in the gut, it's important to make sure the foods that you eat promote good gut health. It's also important that you realize that your entire immune system is also manufactured in your digestive track. The other day, My 3-year-old son had a little struggle with his bathroom number 2 visit. So, my son says, "mommy, mommy it hurts, I need probiotics". My wife and I date each other every week and we alternate the who makes the decision as to what we do. We left my son at my mom's house for a few hours. My mom said, "she fixed him something to eat" and my son said "grandma is healthy". Our children monitor most of what we do, without you ever realizing it. I'm not going to go much further with the probiotics, but my wife and I are consistent with taking them on a daily basis, to optimize our gut functions and prevent leaky gut syndrome. If you wonder why these issues never existed when you were younger, please realize that the acidity levels in our stomach decreases as we get older. Foods that eat are not digested and metabolized properly. Enzymes necessary for proper nutritional extraction become compromised. Stress is another culprit because it increases cortisol levels. I know this is a relationship book, but many people have no idea how something as simple as gut health and an abundance of good microbes has an impact on your mood every day. I'm going to use this opportunity to transition to level three, that is, falling in love or the attachment phase. When a man falls in love, his testosterone levels actually drop and his oxytocin levels increase. The reason for this is because oxytocin is a neurotransmitter responsible for bonding. If I'm with my son, I'm the number one in his life until my wife enters the room. My wife says, "honey, he loves you too". I said, "I know honey, but I can never compete with the level of oxytocin that you exude when you gave birth". This is why in most cases; a man could never compete with a mother and child bond during the incipient stages of

PHYSIOLOGY OF ATTRACTION

life. When two people fall in love to the point where they can't sleep or eat, I assure you that oxytocin levels are surely the blame. I believe that having a firm understanding of the biological effect of good relationship health has helped me to navigate in my relationship as well. When a relationship starts to peak, chemically the ride going up is almost effortless. I call it "the autopilot phase". I assure you, that if you are in a quality relationship and had the opportunity to fall in love with another person, it happens to you as well. Keeping love operating at optimum levels requires basic understanding of all the moving parts and full commitment. When love starts to unravel at the seams and lose chemical bond, all you have to do is follow the path backwards. Oxytocin which supports bonding and being together, followed by Serotonin which impacts mood, and feelings. Dopamine is responsible for anticipation, motivation, and desire. It's currently spring time and our great nation is fighting an evil monster called the Corona virus. My wife has me watching about 6 movies a day to absorb time. While she was preparing a new movie, I quietly went into the backyard unnoticed. I spent about an hour cultivating a small portion of my yard with my tiller. I have become more conscious of agriculture after realizing a spike in cancer rates and its association with hundreds of preservatives placed in our food products to increase shelf life. Agriculture is represented in about 35 different bible verses. The prefix "Agri" in Latin means "land" and "cult" comes from the Latin word "cultus" which means "worship". So, the soil is basically a "LANDCULT" or "LANDWORSHIP". When I first started, I use to buy a bunch of seeds from Home Depot, dig a hole, throw seeds in the ground, water every day and hoping that something happens. Three years later after countless failures, I have come to realize that all seeds are not conducive to all soils. This is why you don't see orange trees in Maryland or Coffee beans being grown in Idaho. It is important that you realize that all energies are not conducive to all people. It just depends on the soil composition. You can be the nicest person in the world and have your energy and time invested in toxic

RECIPROCITY

soil that does not give you the support and strength for proper germination of your ideas, promotions, travel, investments, etc. The reason I love this book so much is because it helps us identify key relationship markers so that you are not wasting time cultivating your garden with people who do not reciprocate your energy regardless of what you do. Now when I go to Home Depot to buy seed for my garden, I realize that I have to buy seed that are conducive to my soil composition. Professional farmers often get their soil tested before planting to see if the soil is depleted of necessary minerals. We must learn from this process and pay strict attention to the soil test during those first dates. Every date leaves a fingerprint as to what's to come in the future. These identifiers are often overlooked because the hormones and neurotransmitters cause us to be more accommodating to deficiencies. We are wired and programed by our creator to bond for propagation. If you take two seeds of an oak tree and place one in a flower pot and the other in a small spot in your yard. You will see over time that the seed that was planted in the yard will grow 100 times the size of the tree that you planted in the large flower pot. The reason for this is because a tree's root system is typically equal to its upper growth for stability. The seed planted in the flower pot's growth is impeded because its environment will not accommodate its potentials. I remember in my engineering class, I learned that the height of a building only goes as high as the some of its base. Are you married or in love with someone with a small flower pot? If you are dating someone that's complacent and content with life and you are not. Hard choices need to be made. In other words, do they complement your thinking, uplift your thoughts, empower your ideas, and pick you up when you need strength. I have to drill this point because as I said earlier in the book. Relationships don't end because of the lack of love they end because of the lack of intimacy. It's sad but some relationships are in competition with each other because they identify money as a means to establish domestic power and as a result look to oppress their mates so they become dependent upon them.

Oftentimes, these relationships have a relatively short shelf life as a result of chronic insecurities. The relationship will eventually starve chemically due to its inability to self-produce sustainable levels of (DOSE) Dopamine, Oxytocin, Serotonin and Endorphins. I believe that we all have a responsibility to maintain good mental and physical health to our partners, because after all this is what we sold. How would you like to buy a $1000 wash machine like my wife had me buy the other day and have many of the functions fail a day after the warranty expired.? Well, your relationships are no different. It's your responsibility to maintain your relationship's warranty. I will list a few things that I do daily to help me uphold my warranty. Also, I want you to buy a container of "Beyond Tangy Tangerine" from a company named "Youngevity". This is one of the only companies I know that has a powdered multivitamin that contains 90 essential vitamins and nutrients. Remember that our body does not crave food, our bodies crave nutrients. Food is nothing more than a vehicle for transport. When you provide the body with proper nutrients, the intestines and stomach have special receptors that send messages to the brain that they are satisfied. If you focus on nutrition rather than eating more food not only will, you have an easier time maintaining and losing weight. Consistent exercise routines will accelerate this process as well. Take a walk in the park, if possible, not on the street. The street causes the brain to process its surroundings that may include sirens, cars, buses, horns, arguments, and could inadvertently elevate cortisol levels unnecessarily which defeats the purpose. The parks typically have nothing but nature. Never assume the fact that you may have put on significant weight that, it's acceptable by your partner. We all have responsibilities to maintain our health because it is what we sold when we got together.

Technology Policy

One of the things I find most interesting with many relationships is the fact that most people are oblivious or reluctant to talk about how they will manage access to their emails, cell phones, online banking, social media accounts, cloud storage drive, and so on. The "baby boomers and generation X'ers", if they attempted to organize their life, operated from a file cabinet or stacked bills on the dining room table which had so many bills, that you had to move them over just to eat dinner. Utility bills, car payments, and mortgage statements because there was no personal computer, cell phone, emails, cloud storage accounts, or social media accounts to store information. Today's population has most of their life on a cell phone, social media, and cloud storage accounts. As a result, technology has literally changed the way that we live. The pandemic has forced many corporations to make adjustments to maintain production levels with their employees working from home. The introduction to 5G will accelerate this trend to the point that commuting to work and working in the office will be in the form of an avatar on our computer screens. Many aspects of our social habits are antiquated and never adjusted to the changing digital times. I know of a couple where the husband died in a car accident and his wife was trying to prepare for his funeral and only 30 people showed up, 25% of them were employees of the funeral home. She did not have any of her husband's family or friend's phone numbers. The funeral was the next week and the phone company indicated that it could only release his contacts with a court order. I realize there other more aggressive things that could be done, but she wanted to do it the right way without partaking in some of the insidious and sinister internet options. I know of another couple where the husband was hit while riding his motorcycle. His family was upset at his wife because she did not notify them. She said I did not have anyone's information because she did not have access to her husband's phone. Once the news circulated, several women who claim to be his active girlfriend showed up at the hospital for quite a surprise. Human arrogance in assuming that tomorrow is promised could lead you down a path of despair and embarrassment. I once mentioned in a class that I authored the book titled, "the psychology of real estate". If you think about it. Everything that we considered owning in life is actually a lease with no option to buy. When we die, everything we owned is repossessed by our creator. I understand the process of inheritance, but my point is that you no longer have it. The difference with the lease that one may have on a house or car is very similar. We have a commencement date or birth date that we all know, but in a lease on life, only your God determines your eviction date. How can we be so arrogant to assume that you are guaranteed another day? Technology should be a primary subject when you've reached a point in a relationship when you think that things are getting serious enough that marriage is a possibility. No, I am not suggesting the fact that you have been dating a man or woman for 6 months that you should be concerned about sharing digital access information. This could be dangerous because there are lots of imposters who represent themselves as good people. This would be pre-mature and neither one of you has been fully vetted. When this elevates to the point that you are considering becoming exclusive and there is possible talk about living together, I find it healthy to at least share phone access and email. I have found that most but not all of the people I know that refuse to share the same phone bill or provide access to their partners have a game. My wife and I started to practice this once we became exclusive. I literally emptied my pockets in front of her with a list of everything that I owned and placed it on the table.

That included bank accounts, business accounts, personal accounts, phone bills, social media accounts, etc. She said, "why are you doing this?" I said tomorrow is not promised and it's my responsibility to ensure that life without me is as seamless as possible. Besides, I realize that I can never get all the love that you have to offer if I don't first give you access to all aspects of my life. True love should never allow materialism to manipulate its decision-making. If I lose something as a result of a bad relationship then I will make it back, but I refuse to love in fear. If we remove the cloud cover off our horizon, every day is always sunny. Let's look at the alternative. You meet someone interesting and one year later the question arises. Where do we go from here? You guys decide to make wedding plans and talk about religion, kids, travel, income, location to live, and left out the technology policy. Subsequently, she notices a pattern that he never answers his phone in her company. She never had his passwords to anything. In fact, she has no idea of anything he does, and neither does he have of hers. As chemical entanglement subsides, doubt into his life starts to creep like a weed in the grass and you finally pay close attention in greater detail. You love him but there are some brain cells that still have doubt about his activity that interrupts some aspects of your conscious thinking. He notices that sex is becoming passionless and predictable. In fact, sex for you is becoming more of a task than an enjoyment. One of the reasons is that your conscious mind is not satisfied with all the data that it has collected and it refuses to completely liberate you because you suspect that your husband has another life on his phone. I'm not insinuating that he was doing anything wrong in the first place. In the next section, I'm going to put this in caps because it's very important. In his defense he never changed, you just thought he would. Your lack of desire to satisfy him causes him to become more vulnerable to external forces and as a result, he made a bad decision and got entangled in a physical relationship with the receptionist at the office. This is a process of reciprocity working in reverse. Back to my wife, she later told me that my decision to surrender and give access was one of the main reasons she said I do. She said, "any man that relinquishes control for the sake of transparency the way that I did understands that integrity and love have an interdependent relationship". Let me quickly divulge the word interdependent because it's important that my readers realize that my choice of words have serious meanings. One day, I was talking to my son and he asked, "why is your company named Fusion?" That led to a dialogue about the composition of the sun. I said the sun is composed of 98% hydrogen and helium. This is the reason the sun never burns out because hydrogen and helium have an interdependent relationship that's necessary for survival. Nuclear Fusion brings energy together and Nuclear Fission tears it apart. Nuclear bombs are Fission based and the sun is Fusion based. For a relationship to survive, three basic elements of Love, Integrity, and Innovation must always be present. The absence of any one of the three will cause the flame to go out. This is where reciprocity reveals itself. I never brought up the subject on if she was going to change her name after we were married. I never made it a requirement or a condition but left it for her to make. In fact, it feels a lot better when someone makes selfless decisions that are non-conditional. The next day, we returned from our honeymoon, and she said, "honey, I have to make some runs be back later this afternoon." I asked her where she was going. She said I'm going to get my name, ID, bank accounts, social security card, and driver's license changed to Cunningham with no hyphen today, and I'm going to put you down as beneficiary on my accounts". I must be honest, I am not suggesting one over the other, however, my wife and I find it more beneficial and healthier from a relationship perspective that we have 100% transparency with everything we have. We are not perfect and as a result, are always creating relationship amendments as we continue to grow. One night, I arranged for a very special dinner date at a 5-star restaurant on the 49th floor of a hotel looking over the harbor. The drive from our home is approximately 1 hour. My wife was on the phone for a half into our drive with a girlfriend until I

TECHNOLOGY POLICY

pulled over on the side of the road. She asked, "why are you stopping?" I said our date started when we left the house not when we get there. I'm not sharing my date time with anyone, that's why my phone is off. Cellphones have become the new relationship kryptonite. I see so many couples who spend more time posting irrelevant content on social media seeking "likes" for validation when they should be seeking validation from the person in their life. We wonder why seven years the relationship has no more fire and juice. My wife and I share the same phone password and she knows my social media passwords as well and we share the same phone account, etc. I find extreme comfort in the fact that if I ever became ill, the primary person in my life can access business associates and family members, accounts, apps, etc. I have a one-click button on a cloud that has full up-to-date instructions with insurance policies, banking, investment ideas, and more to help ease the stress of not having me. I know it's hard because I know people who have lost thousands from their significant others who have taken money without their knowledge and left them in financial ruins. The answer is not to be less transparent with the next relationship but rather to focus on the vetting process and not overlooking the simple things. They say that our personality is fully developed by the age of 7. So, who we are today is exactly who we were at the age of 7? The only thing that has changed are our agendas, behaviors, and habits. My wife and I were out with a couple for dinner and I excused myself from the table and asked my wife to hold my cellphone and answer it if I received a call. The couple found this action bizarre from their perspective because this was something that was forbidden in their relationship. Many couples have expressed the fact that if you have trust, it does not really matter. My argument with this approach is that cellphones probably contain 95% of everything we daily. Trust can't predict if you get in a bad car accident or other health emergency and pertinent information contained in the phone is needed. Let's pause here for a moment and ask you, provided you are in an active relationship. If something were to happen to your spouse or loved one, would you be able to reach their family, friends, business associates, insurance policies, bank accounts, social media, etc. without a court action? If the answer is no, you may be involved in what I call a "technology-induced clandestine relationship". My son and I jog about 12 miles a week. I give him access, just in case, I become incapacitated. In fact, I wish I could have my wife answer all my calls and keep them. Personally, there are individuals I know that don't give their partners access because there are in an inappropriate relationship that they chose to not let go of. I understand both sides of the argument and realize that we have somethings in life that you just want to keep private. May I make a suggestion, buy a diary app for your phone and place a code on it for just you. This way, you still have privacy over your things whatever that may be, and access to the rest of your life is still possible to the people in your life that matter. They deserve it, if you don't like it then why get married and leave someone that you suppose to love with all of this crap to deal with after you are no longer here. Let me just go on record and disclose the fact that my study has revealed that 70% of the couples who have an established technology transparency policy seem to have healthier relationships. I know couples who don't have a technology policy that seem to also have healthy relationships but the majority of the ones who don't, seem to be more challenged. Let me use an analogy I created over the years to explain some reasons behind my point. Let's assume that the love for your partner is represented in an 8oz drinking glass filled with water one for her and another for him. For me to receive all of my wife's love, I must first empty my glass of all 8 oz of water. If I were to leave 2 oz in the glass, I could only receive 6 oz from her. I have found that the more vulnerable I am the more intense her love becomes. Most people don't empty their glass because they are afraid of being hurt. This can only be achieved with complete transparency. I to put this in caps because it's that important. "YOU WILL NEVER RECEIVE LOVE AT THE LEVEL THAT YOU DESIRE IF ASPECTS OF YOUR LIFE ARE PROHIBITED

TO YOUR MATE". The other day, a business associate shared with me that his wife accessed his phone when he was in the shower and questioned him about a woman that called his phone. His position was that she inappropriately answered his phone and therefore did not feel he needed to tell her who this person was. He asked, "Edward what would you have done?" I said, "first of all we have different technology policies. I have one and you don't. My wife has my authority to answer my phone anytime she chooses but she never does because that she does have access. It is actually the opposite effect that most people expect". I said, "have you ever heard the old saying curiosity killed the cat?" Well I eliminated it. I asked him, "why don't you just give her access to your damn cellphone?" he said, "are you kidding?" I answered, "No, In fact, I predict that her love and passion for you will increase to a level that you never experienced before". He said, "Edward, what is your rationale for this logic?" I said, "a woman's love often operates off the principles of certainty". When she knows she has all of you without any restrictions, she will release all bounded-up energy that is seeking to be exposed. Let me ask you a simple question, after which I proceed to end the chapter. Why does your wife not have access to your phone, email, and social media". He said, "We just never talked about it and now it's been over 6 years" I said "you know Mya Angelo once said "our parents did what they knew how to do and when they knew better, they did better". Take your wife to dinner and say, "honey, I love you so much, we are getting older. I think it's important that we share access and passwords as a precaution as part of our estate planning". This is where maturity reveals itself. We have to understand that maturity is not determined by one's chronological achievements, but rather it's determined by one's decision making. If my wife stresses over anything besides that, I'm no longer here, it means that I have failed as a husband to make the necessary lifestyle changes that will ensure a seamless transition to a life without me. How do we commit our entire life to another human being by walking down the aisle, sleep in the same bed, have children, take vacations together, and eat the same food but wait one moment you can't have access to my phone because this is only my business? That's absolute BS. The interesting thing is the fact that my wife rarely accesses my phone because there has never been a reason to. If you love, her the way you say you do then give her your love by relinquishing power and control. Let me clarify my point, people will often say things like you must have trust and does it matter. 57% of marriages ended last year because of trust or money issues. I would estimate that 50% of the 57% ended as a result of information discovered from technology devices. I realize that some partners in relationships can't handle full access because it leads to consistent interrogation on, daily and may have elements of insecurity. Again, I'm not suggesting that all relationships that must have technology policies are in less love than the other. My research suggests that the majority that does not have one have more challenges. I believe trying to keep lust and excitement in your relationship is where your focus should always be. 'The failure to do so could lead to the demise of your relationship.

Ladies and Gentlemen

Someone once asked me, what is the fundamental difference between a lady and a woman. One of the dictionary's definitions of a lady is a woman who is refined, polite, and well-spoken. The dictionary definition of a gentleman is chivalrous, courteous, and honorable. One's socio-economic status is not a prerequisite for being a lady or a gentleman, because it's more of a mindset. I once took a public speaking class years ago and I remember the instructor saying you should always dress to what you aspire to not the position you currently own. If you work in the mailroom when you take off your apron walk to your car in a suit. The reason I have to say this is because our body and mind always gravitate in a direction of our most dominant thoughts. If you think pessimistically then doubt will treat you like a cancer. If you keep attracting people who are parasitic and pessimistic, you should do a self-evaluation of what you see in the mirror because someone is sending out invitations daily. Someone once told me, "Edward, you always have a positive outlook on life". I said, "I have no choice because complaining never seems to work". As a result, over the past years of dating, I typically attracted women who had a positive outlook on life. Negativity always needs a partner because it's difficult to be mad at yourself. I guess this is where the adage "misery loves company" comes from. I know you are wondering where am I going with this, considering that this is a chapter about ladies and gentlemen. For starters, remember that attitude determines altitude. In other words, our circumstances don't dictate our attitude but rather our attitude dictates our circumstances.

I have to establish from time to time that I do have challenges and obstacles in my relationship like anyone else. If I didn't, it would be unrealistic. My wife was going out to a popular venue to celebrate a friend's birthday. I would estimate that 90% of the women were single. After getting ready, she walked out of the bedroom and asked, "honey, how do I look?" I said you look absolutely ravishing and stunning. She had on a mini dress form fitting slightly above the knee, 4inch heels, a white blouse, and cleavage for days. I realized that there is often feminine comradery and she wants to spice up for the group. She said, "do you think I should wear it?" I said, "it is not my attempt to control what you wear, but I'm personally not agreeable to it". She said, "tell me why". I said, a woman will often make decisions in a relationship based on what best represents herself, but a lady makes a decision based on how she represents her family. A woman can still be sexy and also be classy. I'm not suggesting that what you have on is not classy but the amount of cleavage and the skirt makes you look too exposed. Some outfits give the perception that we are auditioning and it may not be the best representation of our union. "Honey, if any of my guy friends were to see you, they would immediately wonder if we were still together". Many single women believe that dressing overly sexy is attractive. Most men would probably agree and that's primarily because men since the beginning of time have always had an appetite for eye candy and it will never end. It's a fundamental element of human nature. What you package yourself as is what you will attract. Do you want to be the eye candy or do you want to be the box? I think the answer lies in your agenda. The box is more desirable than the candy because of the way that it's packaged. When a gentleman is looking for someone to coexist in a domestic capacity, he is typically more interested in the box rather than the candy. He looks at the detail in the ribbons, reads the packaging, and wraps to get a feel for its character and integrity. Men often make decisions based on what they see, but gentlemen make decisions based on what they see and hear. I read an interesting

RECIPROCITY

article the other day and that indicated that 56.8 million women are single in the US. I know of several women who would love to be married. They all earn over 100K a year, own a home, and have solid reserves. I suggested, why don't you familiarize and immerse yourself with something you're not used to. If you desire to meet a gentleman who knows how to treat a lady. Why don't you expose yourself to new hobbies and endeavors where the odds of meeting that type of person exist? Equestrian events, art shows, entrepreneur business conferences, join a non-profit, women's church retreats, and the likes. I'm tired of hearing women say where are all the good men. The answer could be in the venues that you frequent. Evening classes at your local community college in order to increase the odds. What kind of man is in the library on a Saturday afternoon? What kind of man is at the playground with his daughter because it's his weekend to have her? Do you think you are going to meet the man of your dreams at happy hour every week with a girlfriend at the local bar? You can't buy a new Porsche at a fiat dealership. If all women decided collectively that they wanted a rugged and resourceful gentleman today, men would change in about a week. Women have so much influence on what a man does with his money and time. Conversely, some men wish to have a wife but never focused on the fact that their childish characteristics of having an overzealous mother who coddled him profusely created a man who does not have adequate masculine energy to give his woman comfort. A true gentleman always sacrifices his needs to give to others. He's nice and respected but has a swagger to kick ass if needs to protect his family. He does not play child games when it comes to domestic integrity. He always monitors his income to give his wife economic flexibility. He does not cheat, he's spiritual, religious, and dates his wife consistently on non-holidays, He gets his wife flowers every week and administers consistent love, affection, attention, and praise. Although they have been together for 7 years, he makes love to her like they just met.

This man is where the shortage lies. When I talk about this man to my feminine readers, their eyes light up. This is because giving to herself is truly a gift to him. Always making assessments on how to be a better person. I know of a married couple that my wife and I are familiar within our business. I told my wife that she's not happy. She said, "how do you know honey"? I just spoke to her a week ago and she said the family is fine. I said, "honey, you know we can speak without talking and move without walking. She has a change in patterns from when we first met them. Her attire gives me the impression that she's auditioning for new opportunities because this is the way that she dresses in the absence of her husband. This is significantly different from the earlier days. 3 months later her husband finds out that she is having an affair. I was joking with my wife the other day and said you know what I've noticed. I said like clockwork you can almost calculate how long a couple has been together based on the distance that they walk apart when getting out of the car walking across a parking lot to the mall for example. New couples are always in parallel holding hands and appear to be inseparable. In a 2-year-old relationship, men typically walk a few feet ahead. Couples who have been together for 20 plus years meet their wives in the store after they park the car. It's funny but it's true. My calculations are about 1 foot of distance per year together. It's not that they are not happy but rather the parties have become complacent in the things that got them together. In conclusion, of this chapter please remember that we always through reciprocity attract who we are. Women attract Men and Ladies attract Gentlemen. Discover yourself and determine what's right for you. I want to also add clarity to the fact that love is not like pregnancy, meaning you are either pregnant or you're not. I believe that the love intensity can be spread out on a scale 1-7. When two people fall in love you will often hear people refer to the fact that they have been married three times but she loved john more. I don't doubt the fact that she fell in love with all three but john had qualities that were far more superior than the others. I will leave this chapter with an amazing quote that I created. "The true measure of a man is not based on the things that he may accumulate in a lifetime but rather in the smile of the woman that stands by him".

Laws of Zero

Remember in the first grade when we started refining our math skills, we learned that any number when added to zero remains that number. Well, in relationships our math skills are just as important. My wife cleans the house, I cut the grass, and clean the pool. My wife washes the clothes. I wash all the cars. These are some of the examples of her physical contributions. She gives me the intellectual sparing and debate that allows me to continue to grow as a person. Here is the fundamental question you need to ask yourself. If your partner left you for 90 days, what would you miss the most from their contributions? Before you answer the question, take out the number of things you would miss and add them up. If you get to 15 out of 20 consider yourself very lucky. If you have a score of 20 out of 20, it is not favorable either because that could mean that he or she is overindulging and this could make you more dependent on their presence. If you don't miss anything, then it's possible that their contributions could only be a zero. My wife has a friend that's engaged. This woman complains every time my wife has a general conversation with her. She constantly complains about her fiancée. He does work consistently and pays a small utility bill, all of his other time is spent playing video games. He does not clean, wash, cook, cut grass, spend time with their children. Also, they have not gone on dates or no vacations for several years. My wife told her to take the small "Laws of Zero" quiz. Well, his relationship contribution score was a zero. If you have someone in your life that you fail to miss in their absence, the number will speak for itself. Your situation has to be addressed otherwise you have to make a self-evaluation as to why you are consistently facilitating this abuse. You have become an enabler of bad habits because you never set parameters and enforced them with consistency. Now bad patterns have evolved into bad habits. I know the common narrative will be "but I still love him or her." You know it's possible to love someone that you don't necessarily like. Now the person who overindulges in a relationship to compensate for what their partners are not doing could cause depression and lead to a burnt-out relationship. If the number is too high, this could also be a problem. The question that many people have is, "how could that be?" I said you have to understand that overindulgence is one of the most insidious forms of abuse. This is the man that is so insecure that he will say, "Honey, I don't want you to lift a finger, I have everything covered. All I want you to do is breathe". This man strips you quietly from contribution so that your entire life is dependent upon him. This way, he gets to control the narrative because you have no significant contribution. If you have no contribution, then everything that you do has to come from him, and this gives him the control that he desires. Be very careful with this situation because you must remember that fear is the father of anger. This is fine if it is what you want, but let me warn you, it could be catastrophic in the end. This woman is totally oblivious to everything and is often left with nothing because she knows nothing. My daughter started a job as a high school senior working with Chipotle near her school. The first thing I told her was to always make her presence missed. She asked why? I said, "…because that's where your value is assessed. Go to work early, leave late. Whatever your responsibility is, make sure you augment the process. If your job is to cut the chicken make that process better. If your job is to cut veggies, make that process better. If you ever decide to leave, they will pay you more to stay because money does not follow people, money only follows value". Well, what happened next was unexpected. The manager was just a few years older than she was and this was their full-time job. The manager was so insecure with the fact that my daughter was offered to go to management classes that she began to reduce her hours to 4 per week so that she would have to get another job. The point that I'm making is that it does not matter the endeavor, always make your presence missed. If you have something in your life that no one else wants get rid of it. If you don't, it's like having extra sandbags on a hot air balloon. This formula can be applied to all aspects of your life. On your job, if they don't miss your presence, I assure you that when it comes down to reducing the budget to save cost, it's possible that you can be expendable. Everything in life that's worth having requires work.

In conclusion, I want to thank you for reading my book on reciprocity. If you have learned one thing that could add value to yourself or your relationship, kindly let me know that the book added value to someone's life. Be sure to download the app **reciprocity,** to help reinforce a lot of the relationship principles that I have outlined in the book. You will find it extremely beneficial in your quest to add value and spice to your existing relationship. 100% of everything that I have disclosed here is what I try to do daily. If you are looking to restore lust, excitement, and juice into your relationship, you have absolutely nothing to lose and everything to gain. There is nothing more dissatisfying than raising a family in a loveless household.

Thank you,
Edward Cunningham
The Author

www.ingramcontent.com/pod-product-compliance
Lightning Source LLC
Chambersburg PA
CBHW070929080526
44589CB00013B/1446